THE COMMONWEALTH ANI

Joint Chairmen of the Honor

SIR ROBERT ROBINSON,

DEAN ATHELSTAN SP

MATHEMATI(

General Editor: C. PLUMPTON

MATHEMATICS WITH UNDERSTANDING

BOOK 1

MATHEMATICS WITH UNDERSTANDING

BOOK 1

Harold Fletcher and Arnold A. Howell

PERGAMON PRESS

Oxford · New York · Toronto · Sydney
Braunschweig

Pergamon Press Ltd., Headington Hill Hall, Oxford
Pergamon Press Inc., Maxwell House, Fairview Park, Elmsford, New York 10523
Pergamon of Canada Ltd., 207 Queen's Quay West, Toronto 1
Pergamon Press (Aust.) Pty. Ltd., 19a Boundary Street,
Rushcutters Bay, N.S.W. 2011, Australia
Vieweg & Sohn GmbH, Burgplatz 1, Braunschweig

First edition 1970
Library of Congress Catalog Card No. 78-111361

Printed in Hungary

08 015656 8 (flexicover)
08 015657 6 (hard cover)

CONTENTS

PREFACE

IN RECENT years many changes have taken place in the content of and the approach to the teaching of mathematics in primary schools. As a result of this it was felt necessary to provide a guide to the new ideas in Primary Mathematics for students in colleges of education. It is hoped that qualified teachers will also find it helpful and thought-provoking. Thus whenever the words teacher or student are used, note that they refer to teachers of mathematics in primary-schools or students in training to be such teachers. For the ease of presentation the subject-matter has been divided into two books. It is unfortunate that some topics, e.g. **Measurement** and **Shape and Size,** had to be placed in Book 2, and it is essential that students and teachers integrate the appropriate sections of both books. We have attempted to present the contents in such a way that will encourage careful analysis of known techniques and constructive discussion between tutor and student or teacher and child as well as increasing the reader's knowledge of the new developments in mathematics.

Set language is used throughout the books. This is not simply to be modern but because of a sincere belief that this is a natural language for children and that it helps them and teachers alike to a deeper understanding of the structure behind many mathematical ideas and processes.

PREFACE

In recent years many changes have taken place in the content and the approach to the teaching of mathematics in primary schools. As a result of this [illegible] mathematics [illegible] [illegible] teachers [illegible] [illegible] of mathematics [illegible] [illegible]

[illegible] and teaching [illegible] [illegible] both books [illegible] [illegible] between [illegible] students [illegible] knowledge of the new [illegible]

Set [illegible] is used throughout the book. [illegible]

CHAPTER 1

THE AIMS OF A MODERN APPROACH

Introduction

WHAT is Mathematics? This question is often asked of students in colleges of education who are not specialists in mathematics but who nevertheless are faced with the prospect of teaching mathematics in primary schools. Often the first answers are concerned with some aspect of Arithmetic. Suggestions are that mathematics deals with computation, with learning mechanical process, with number and so on. This reflects on their memories of primary-school days when often little other than arithmetic was taught in the mathematics lesson. Some remember working with protractors and think of this as geometry, but for the most part arithmetic predominates the thinking. Happily this is not a picture of primary-school mathematics today in most schools though there are still some where long hours are spent practising half-understood techniques. Gradually the student begins to realize that mathematics is not just concerned with number at this level but with relationships of many kinds.

In his book *Prelude to Mathematics* W. W. Sawyer gives as a starting-point for a discussion on the nature of mathematics the following: "Mathematics is the classification and study of all possible patterns." He further stresses that by pattern here is meant any regularity that the mind can recognize. Z. P. Dienes, writing to justify the use of his excellent set of logical blocks, says: "We will not develop children's powers of reasoning if we regard mathematics as a series of mechanical processes to be learned by rote." Some of the aims of the Nuffield Mathematics Experiment for children from 5 years to 13 years have been stated as that of making the children more critical, logical and creative. From these we see that mathematics is concerned with classification, with regularities or patterns, with logic or powers of reasoning, with critical thought and with creativity. The title of a well-known book about mathematics is *Mathematics, Queen and Servant of Science*, and reminds us that mathematics is indeed involved in solving scientific problems and is an important tool of science. It is vital that students and teachers realize that children are deeply involved with mathematics in the primary school and not just with some parts of arithmetic.

We can now proceed to ask a further question. What is the philosophy behind the mathematics of the primary school? It is not easy to give a short answer, and the following "key words", which should be written in blood on the hearts of teachers, may give some guidance. The order in which the words are given is neither one of ascending or descending importance. All are important and worthy of careful thought and long discussions between tutor and student.

Understanding

There are those who assert that children should be taught mathematical techniques or processes as one might teach unskilled operators to press the correct buttons of a machine in the right order. They further assert that understanding as to why the buttons are so manipulated comes only after long hours of weary practice in operating the machine. The authors cannot stress too strongly that they disagree with this point of view. For processes to be used correctly and remembered it is essential that the children have understanding from the beginning.

Consider the following illustration.

ILLUSTRATION

A teacher wishes to help a child arrive at the correct solution of the following problem:

$$\begin{array}{r} 26 \\ +38 \\ \hline \\ \hline \end{array}$$

Sometimes, unfortunately, the instructions proceed thus: Eight and six are fourteen. Put down 4 under the 8 and put a little 1 under the 3. Now say one and three and two are six. Put the 6 down next to the 4. Now do you UNDERSTAND? It is possible that the instructions enable the child to understand *what to do*, but this is vastly different from understanding the structures involved. This kind of instruction is useless.

Discussion point for students and tutors. Is the above a greatly distorted account of some teachers' ways of dealing with the difficulty?

Consider now some of the difficulties of this apparently simple problem. This is an abstract problem in mathematics. Possibly there is a real situation where a collection of twenty-six objects and a completely different set of thirty-eight objects are put together into one large collection. Further it is desired to know how many objects there are altogether. The "putting together" is symbolized by the + and the desire to find how many there were altogether by the space for the required solution.

Note. (a) Children are only able to cope with abstract mathematical symbols and ideas after dealing with concrete situations in which they themselves are interested.

(b) A large variety of similar situations are necessary before abstraction takes place.

Returning to a consideration of the illustration it should be observed that understanding cannot take place unless the child appreciates the STRUCTURE behind the base ten system of recording. The numbers twenty-six and thirty-eight are recorded as 26 and 38 using our base ten system. Had we been born with two fingers and a thumb on each hand instead of four fingers it is probable that we should have used a base six system of recording.

Recording of numbers will be dealt with more fully in Chapter 4, but it might help the reader to appreciate more clearly the child's difficulty if he tries to solve the problem of adding twenty-six to thirty-eight using a base six system of recording.

(*Note*. Some students will argue that it is not possible to have twenty-six objects in base six. They are confusing number names with methods of recording. It is probable that had we been born with two fingers and a thumb we should have had a new name for twenty-six. Discuss this with a fellow student or tutor.)

Students should appreciate firstly that mathematical symbols, e.g. $\div$, often present difficulties; secondly that children, who have been taught a mechanical approach and not been encouraged to think, find it easy to give absurd answers without challenging them and, thirdly, do not usually do the problem by the simplest method involving the least amount of computation. The following examples illustrate these three points.

Example 1. When presented with the simple problem 15 p $\div$ 3 p children often give the result as 5 p.

When this is put into a concrete situation it is clear that the answer is a pure number. One such situation might be: Fifteen new pence is shared between a number of children and each receives 3 new pence. How many children were there?

Example 2. When some children were asked to put the fractions $\frac{1}{3}$, $\frac{1}{4}$, $\frac{1}{2}$, $\frac{1}{5}$ in order of size the following remarks were overheard: "I must find the L.C.M. Is it 120? Do we turn anything upside-down?" If only they had realized that when sharing a cake the smallest piece is obtained by the largest number of cuts, they could have put the fractions in order immediately.

It should be the aim of the teacher to increase the children's power of mathematical thinking and to help them to as complete an understanding of the structure behind the processes as possible. To this end it is considered that situations may have to be devised or contrived to encourage discussion within the field of mathematical thinking being considered at the time.

Structure

This word has been used several times already, e.g. "the structure behind the base ten system of recording". Most of the rest of this book deals with an analysis of the mathematical structures involved in primary-school mathematics. It is therefore pointless giving many examples at this stage to illustrate the meaning of the word. One further example may, however, be helpful.

When a set of two oranges is added to a set of three apples there are five pieces of fruit. The mathematical abstraction of this situation may be recorded as $3+2 = 5$. Had the three apples been added to the two oranges the corresponding abstraction might have been $2+3 = 5$. This is an example of a basic law or rule known as the commutative law of addition. This law may be expressed in algebraic terms by $a+b = b+a$. It is part of the inherent structure of number systems. (The development of the number system will be dealt with more fully in Book 2.) It may be a matter for discussion as to whether the word "commutative" should be part of primary-school vocabulary, but the fact remains that when children are able to appreciate this law (or this bit of structure) the memory work involved in learning the addition number facts is almost halved, for if the result of $8+7$ is known, for example, so is the result of $7+8$.

Discovery

Many years ago mathematics lessons in primary schools were almost invariably spent sitting at desks doing routine problems. Over the years a change has taken place. It is recognized that children often learn by doing. Practical work is essential. Children will only understand the concept of volume after a lot of practical work, e.g. filling containers with water and sand. In this way they discover for themselves which of several containers holds the most and are able to place them in order of size. Length becomes meaningful after children have measured all kinds of objects including the classroom, playground, etc. (Measurement will be dealt with fully in Book 2, but it is worth noting here that estimation is important and that there should be motivation so that the children have a purpose in measuring.)

Much of mathematics is concerned with abstract ideas. In order that children should understand concepts and be able to think in the abstract they need a rich variety of concrete materials to help them. For example, number itself is abstract. It is when a child has handled two oranges, two apples, two dinky toys, two conkers, etc., and when he has seen two hands, two feet, two eyes, etc., that he begins to understand the abstract idea of the twoness of a set of two members. He puts together in one set two apples and three oranges and discovers that he has five pieces of fruit. He has two shells and three shells and finds that he has five shells altogether. At a later stage he is able to think in the abstract and record using the numerals 2, 3 and 5 thus: $2+3 = 5$.

(*Note.* (i) The authors intend this to be read as 2 plus 3 is another way of writing 5. (ii) Number will be dealt with more fully in Chapter 2.)

The role of the teacher must be to create in his classroom a mathematical climate which will help the children in this discovery. On the walls there should be charts which ask questions as well as those giving information. Children's work should be on display and discussed frequently. A number strip should be on the wall. Puzzles, magic squares, etc., must be available. The following is a list, by no means a comprehensive one, of some of the mathematics equipment that should also be available in the junior classroom: string, tape, wool, cotton, tape measures, trundle wheels, metre rules, home-made clinometers, containers of all kinds, sand, water, liquid measures, funnel, rubber tubing, sieve, shapes which will tessellate, three-dimensional models made from pipe cleaners and straws, nail boards with a square lattice and with circles, multiboards, mosaic shapes, Dienes' logical blocks, elastic bands, peg board, real money (if possible), shop materials, balances, weights, spring balances, household scales, bathroom scales, assorted parcels of different weights, plasticine, printed number squares, abacus, lengths of card cut for use with the number strip, graph paper, coloured paper and gummed coloured paper, egg-timers, pulsometers, stop-watch, Smiths' pinger, wooden or cardboard clocks with movable hands.

Three points should be borne in mind.

(i) It is probable that if left entirely to himself the child will discover very little. The teacher must be perpetually creating situations where discovery can take place. Sometimes directed questions will be needed and sometimes more open questions will allow children to develop particular interests. Discussion is vital if discovery is to take place. (This will be considered in the next section.)

(ii) Discovery does not only take place when the child is doing some practical work. It can take place when he is at his desk exercising his powers of thought. He can be led to discover new processes, new techniques and to clarify his ideas.

As part of an experiment, a class of first-year Juniors was asked to talk about the window pane and to see what mathematics they could discover from it. The experiment was repeated with some 10-year-olds. Part of the discussion went as follows:

Mathematics derived from observing a window pane (first-year Juniors)

"It's got an axis of symmetry down the middle."

"If you fold it, one side is the same as the other."

"You can't fold a window but a piece of paper is the same shape."

"It's a rectangle or an oblong, whichever you like to call it."

"You can fold it the other way as well."

"You can fold it corner to corner."

Chorus: "No! You would do it with a square but not a rectangle."

"If you cut it corner to corner it would be the same, but if you fold it, it isn't."

"I mean fold it diagonally. It's the diagonal that makes two triangles. They are right-angled triangles because of the corner. It's 90°. A right angle can be turned into a square."

"You could measure all the sides."

Class Teacher: "What name do we give to the measurement of all the sides together?"

"If I look in my book I'll be able to find out. – Perimeter!"

"It has two top sides and two long sides that measure the same. That is two pairs."

"When it's a square you can fold the diagonal and it's an axis of symmetry."

"You wouldn't have so many centimetres on one axis as the other in a rectangle."

"If you turn it, it's like a kite or a diamond."

"I bet you didn't think you would get all this!"

CLASS 7. CHILDREN 10 YEARS OF AGE

"It has length and width."
"The pane of glass has three dimensions."
"LOOK AT THE SURFACE."
"The surface is part of a plane."
"What Must It Have?"
"The surface has the property of area."
"It is congruent with the next pane."
"The measure of the angles is two straight angles."
"Each corner has an angle measurement of 90°."
"It has a rectangle shape."
"It is a quadrilateral."
"It is transparent."
"It has two lines of symmetry."
"When folding on these lines of symmetry they will fold exactly."

Class Teacher: "How many ways can I put the pane in the window?"
"Four, because it's transparent."
"You can manoeuvre it in different ways. You can move it through a turn which I can measure in degrees."
"The window handle is like the hand of a clock. You can rotate it through a measurement of 360°."
"The opposite sides are the same length and parallel."
"The piece of glass is a cuboid."

Class Teacher: "Is it a rectangular prism?" "Yes."

(iii) The above experiment showed how the environment of the child could be used for discovery and discussion.

A few other examples are:

(a) use of leaves, etc., from the nature table for discoveries of relationships of all kinds, e.g. symmetry, numbers and lengths of veins, length of main stalk, length of leaf, area and perimeter relationships;

(b) use of model cars and other scale models for discoveries about proportion;
(c) use of tile flooring for tessellations;
(d) use of clockwork trains and traffic passing the school for ideas about speed and statistics.

Discussion

Every opportunity for discussing mathematics with children should be taken. Often this will be with individual children or small groups of children who are working together on a particular project that they are interested in. There is still a place for discussion with a whole class on some occasions. Opportunities may arise in the following ways. Firstly, the subject of mathematics is ever growing and so too does the child's knowledge of the subject develop and grow. There may be times when a child is faced with a situation which he is keen to solve. He calls upon his past experiences and knowledge in an attempt to solve the new situation. It is at this point that the teacher must be prepared to discuss with the child. The task then confronting the teacher is not an easy one. He must choose between leading and allowing the child to lead. He must know when to guide and when to leave the child alone with his thoughts. It is probable that the teacher knows what possibilities for discovery there are in the situation. Discussion may lead to discovery. It has previously been stated that situations may have to be devised to facilitate discovery. Discussion is vital in this respect. The wise teacher knows also when to allow discussion to explore unexpected avenues.

Secondly, it is often only when discussion has taken place that the teacher knows when a particular technique or particular aspect of mathematical structure is known. Many readers will remember the seemingly endless practice of types of "sums" when they were in the primary school. (They were often called "sums" though in fact often they were not for the word "sum" is understood to mean addition.) It has already been stated that merely doing twenty, thirty or more routine examples of half-understood techniques is useless. Discussion with the child is one of the ways, possibly the only way, whereby the teacher knows whether a particular technique is fully understood or not. When, after discussion, the teacher is convinced that there is understanding, then of course *it is necessary to practice*. Children must be as efficient as possible and need some practice. The question to be asked is how little practice is needed to maintain efficiency. This difficult question can only be answered for each individual child by each individual teacher using his experience. Perhaps research is needed too. It is certainly true that too much practice leads to boredom, to a dislike of mathematics and even to a loss of efficiency.

The following true story may help to emphasize this point. A student on teaching practice had been asked by the school to "teach" long multiplication. "The children know their nine times table," he told his tutor. The problem of evaluating 9×35 was discussed and the following possible way of recording to promote understanding suggested.

We require nine thirty-fives.

$$\begin{array}{rl} 35 & \\ 9 & \\ \hline 45 & \rightarrow \text{This is 9 fives.} \\ 270 & \rightarrow \text{This is 9 thirties.} \\ \hline 315 & \rightarrow \text{This is 9 thirty-fives.} \\ \hline \end{array}$$

The student was convinced that this was too difficult for the children. "They will never understand that way," he said. He further went on to say that the children could already do the example if one said to them something like:

Nine fives are forty-five. Put down five and carry four. Put a small four down to help you remember. Now say nine threes are twenty-seven and four is thirty-one. The recording would be:

$$\begin{array}{r} 35 \\ {\scriptstyle 4}\ 9 \\ \hline 315 \\ \hline \end{array}$$

The fact was that the student himself had never really understood the underlying structure known as the distributive law nor even had a firm grasp of the structure behind the base ten system of recording. He was able to perform the tricks but no amount of practice had led to understanding. Discussion between tutor and student was necessary.

Note to students. Please discuss the above situation with your tutor. It is not exaggerated in any way.

Further consideration of the above problem of finding 9×35 leads on to another key word, namely, flexibility.

Flexibility

One of the aims of mathematics teaching in the primary school is that of encouraging children to think clearly and to develop their powers of reasoning. All too often a set way of doing a particular problem is given to children. Instead they should be encouraged to use a variety of methods. These can be discussed so that the children choose the method most appropriate to the occasion.

Remember:

It is better to do one thing in three ways than to do three things in one way.

Or: One thing—many ways—sometimes.

Thus there are many opportunities in the classroom when it is useful to ask children to do a certain problem in as many ways as they can. The bright child may find seven or eight ways, the average child three or four and the weak ones possibly two. In this way all children benefit by working at their own level. Group or class discussions of interesting solutions are well worth while.

The reader may like to find several ways of evaluating the previous problem, viz. 9×35.

Here are three possibilities:

(i) $10 \times 35 = 350$ and hence $9 \times 35 = 350 - 35 = 315$.

(ii) $2 \times 35 = 70$,

$4 \times 35 = 2 \times 70 = 140$

$8 \times 35 = 2 \times 140 = 280$

Hence $9 \times 35 = 280 + 35 = 315$.

(iii) $9\times 35 = 9\times(7\times 5) = (9\times 7)\times 5 = 63\times 5$

$= (60\times 5)+(3\times 5)$

$= 300+15 = 315.$

Example for the reader:

How many ways of evaluating $6\frac{1}{2}\times 7\frac{1}{2}$ can you discover? A number of students were asked to try the above question. The first solution offered by almost all of them was:

$$6\tfrac{1}{2}\times 7\tfrac{1}{2} = \tfrac{13}{2}\times\tfrac{15}{2} = \tfrac{195}{4} = 48\tfrac{3}{4}.$$

Incidentally pencil and paper was needed for the step $13\times 15 = 195$ in most cases, which was done using the standard long multiplication method of recording.

Three other possible solutions are given to provoke discussion.

(i) $2\times 6\frac{1}{2} = 13$ and so $8\times 6\frac{1}{2} = 52.$

$\frac{1}{2}\times 6\frac{1}{2} = 3\frac{1}{4}.$

Hence $7\frac{1}{2}\times 6\frac{1}{2} = 52-3\frac{1}{4} = 48\frac{3}{4}.$

(ii) $6\times 7\frac{1}{2} = 3\times 15 = 45$

$\frac{1}{2}\times 7\frac{1}{2} = 3\frac{3}{4}.$

Hence $6\frac{1}{2}\times 7\frac{1}{2} = 45+3\frac{3}{4} = 48\frac{3}{4}.$

(*Note.* This method might have been suggested if the problem had been that of finding the cost of $6\frac{1}{2}$ m of ribbon at $7\frac{1}{2}$ p per m.

i.e. 2 m for 15 p $\Rightarrow$ 6 m for 45 p

$\frac{1}{2}$ m for $3\frac{3}{4}$ p leading to

$6\frac{1}{2}$ m for $48\frac{3}{4}$ p which would be corrected to 50 p since

$\frac{1}{4}$ np is not a legal unit.)

(iii) If cm squared paper were available then the following diagram would help in the solution. The problem would then have been that of finding how many squares there are in $6\frac{1}{2}$ rows when there are $7\frac{1}{2}$ squares in a row.

The solution might read $42+3+3\frac{1}{2}+\frac{1}{4} = 48\frac{3}{4}$.

The reader should compare this with:

$$\left(6+\tfrac{1}{2}\right)\times\left(7+\tfrac{1}{2}\right) = (6\times7)+\left(6\times\tfrac{1}{2}\right)+\left(\tfrac{1}{2}\times7\right)+\left(\tfrac{1}{2}\times\tfrac{1}{2}\right)$$

or with: $(a+b)\times(c+d) = ac+ad+bc+bd.$

Note. Flexibility should not be over-used. It is pointless doing *every* example in many ways.

Remember: One thing—Many ways—Sometimes.

Two further points concerning flexibility should be noted.

(i) Ten questions were given to two sets of children. Of these ten questions nine were of a routine nature and the tenth could be done either by a fairly long routine process or a much shorter neater method. To one set this question was given as the first question and to the other set it was the last question. When it appeared first, a number of the children did it by the shorter, neater method. When it appeared as the last question no child did it by the shorter method. It would seem that after doing nine routine questions they were conditioned to a mechanical process. There would therefore appear to be some evidence for saying that mechanical repetition does not help children to exercise their powers of thought.

(ii) Often when children have discovered how to do a certain process by several methods it is necessary for the teacher to discuss them and to direct the child's attention to a good method. This is not a contradiction of (i) above. Children need practice in using good methods but the question remains as to how little practice is necessary for efficiency. At the same time the child's ability to look for less obvious but more rewarding methods of solution should be encouraged.

Power Skill

This skill is revealed when a child is able to use his knowledge (understanding) to solve a new situation. He calls on past experiences and uses his thinking power gained from those experiences to analyse the new problem. If he has power skill he will attack a problem with some technique and arrive at a solution. It may involve a very long process totally unrelated to traditional techniques—nevertheless this power skill is the key to mathematical progress. In due season, the skilful teacher can lead the child to a more sophisticated technique. Here are examples which may illustrate power skill.

(a) On one occasion, a boy faced with 12 twelves, laid out his array like this:

```
0000000000 | 00
0000000000 | 00
0000000000 | 00
0000000000 | 00
0000000000 | 00
0000000000 | 00
0000000000 | 00
0000000000 | 00
0000000000 | 00
0000000000 | 00
-----------+---
0000000000 | 00
0000000000 | 00
```

He then commented: "I have a set of 100, 4 sets of ten and 4 sets of one, so 12 twelves is $100+40+4 \rightarrow 144$.

"I know we group in H.T.U so this is easier than counting in ones."

He called upon previous knowledge to solve a new situation. This is POWER.

(b) A child who had no knowledge of place value was asked the question: There are 43 children in the class and 29 are going to the baths. How many will remain in the classroom?

He replied, "I can use my counting to tell you. It's the only way I know." He recorded as follows:

$$\begin{array}{l} 29+\ \ 1 \rightarrow 30 \\ 30+10 \rightarrow 40 \\ 40+\ \ \underline{3} \rightarrow 43 \\ \quad\ \ 14 \end{array}$$

Fourteen stay at school.

(c) The children knew tables to 5×5.

A question was asked—9×5?

One boy replied, "We haven't done it yet." Another boy said, "I'll have a try."

"9 is another way of writing 5+4 so instead of 9×5 I could say 5×5, 4×5 and add them.

25 and 20 is 45.

"I say 9×5 is 45. Am I right?"

In all these examples the child calls upon past experience to assist in solving a new situation.

Sometimes the tendency in primary schools has been to concentrate on speed skills. Speed skills do not lead to power skills. Increase the power skills, however, and the speed skills will certainly follow.

Pattern

The evidence of pattern is an essential feature of mathematical thought. The pattern is not a visual one, it is a mental one, the mind seeing a regularity of behaviour. With sequence patterns a rhythm is *felt* and the ability to observe the next member of the regular sequence involves a mental process. This ability grows with the maturing child.

Pattern, in the early years, can be defined as a disciplined classification and is part of the sorting which introduces infants to mathematics at the beginning of their school life. This disciplined sorting arises from a sorting where children add from a random collection to the teacher's set which may be one involving such properties as (say) colour, size, texture.

It is emphasized strongly that insufficient work involving rhythmic sequence is attempted in Infants' schools at present.

For example:

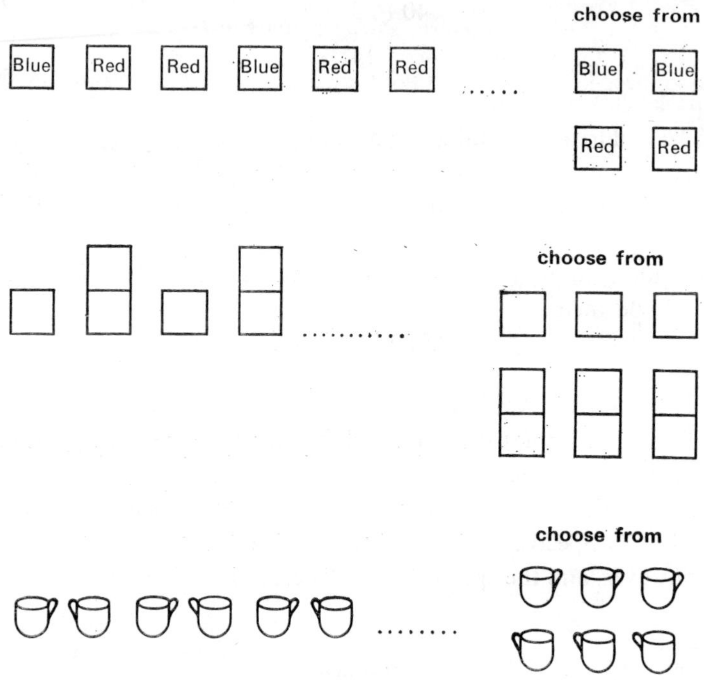

Later pattern (not necessarily a rhythmic sequence) leads to generalization. From the study of solid shapes the generalization of a relationship between vertices, faces and edges (Euler's characteristic) can be "discovered" by very young children.

The use of graphs illustrates pattern. The patterns are presented in visual form and the visual pattern is easy to recognize, but this is insufficient. The child must decide what the pattern is. He must communicate the mental pattern from his observations of the visual. The idea of the same pattern arising in different circumstances is stressed in later years. Perhaps we change the word *pattern* to *structure*. In any case the word *isomorphic* expresses the idea that two things which may be considered as wide apart are mathematically identical.

Pleasure, Purpose and Purity

These three key words are taken together—they can be remembered as the three P's!

Pleasure. Mathematics is not a dead subject. It should be presented as living and dynamic in the classroom. Children enjoy mathematics when they are suitably motivated and are activily engaged in learning. Even less exciting parts of the subject need not be boring. Naturally number facts and tables have to be known but by allowing children to consult copies of tables *which they themselves have built up* wrong solutions and drudgery can be reduced to a minimum. Gradually confidence and competence are gained.

Purpose. There is so much interesting work to be done in the primary school that there is no time nor point in purposeless computation. The reply to the question as to how many halfpennies there are in £16 ought to be "Who cares!" Much of the practice needed for computation can be achieved from examples where the children recognize patterns in the various solutions. The teacher should be able to satisfy himself that there is purpose behind all that is done in the mathematics lessons, e.g. if block graphs are drawn and not used subsequently for descriptive writing, for the formulation and answering of questions and for computation there is little or no purpose in drawing the graph in the first place.

Purity. No slipshod mathematical language and no careless use of symbols should be the aim of every primary school teacher. Unfortunately it is all too true that many teachers are careless in the use of mathematical language. Such terms as "borrow and pay back", "move the decimal point", do not help children to understand structure but in fact lead to misconceptions. Every effort should be made to use language which is mathematically sound and which leads to a better understanding of the particular part of mathematics under consideration.

A friend of the author recalled that when she was about 12 years of age her teacher said: "Remember that a minus times a minus is a plus." "Why?" asked the girl. The reply came, "Because the enemy of your enemy is your friend." The logic of this failed to convince the girl who went on to say, "But the enemy of my enemy is not my friend. In fact the friend of my enemy is not my enemy nor is the enemy of my friend either my friend or my enemy." The only answer the teacher could think of was, "Do be quiet." Beware of such stupid analogies. They serve only to confuse the confused. Discuss with your tutor why slipshod language is used in the primary school.

Here are some suggestions:

(i) It is sometimes a quick way of teaching children to perform the "tricks", i.e. the routine processes. At first the children produce a series of right answers and this lulls the teacher into thinking that there is understanding.

(ii) It is easy to become fixed in one's ways when teaching and to remember and repeat parrot-fashion phrases without considering whether or not they are meaningful.

(iii) There is sometimes a lack of mathematical knowledge on the part of the teacher.

Techniques and Practice

It is important to remember that sound techniques are required and some practice is needed for efficiency. It has been stated already but is repeated for emphasis that the aim sould be to achieve this efficiency by the minimum of practice.

CHAPTER 2

THE LANGUAGE OF SETS

THIS chapter and the first part of Chapter 3 deal largely with the background knowledge which is a necessary part of the primary teacher's store of information. It is not suggested that the whole of this chapter is suitable for the primary school. Symbols have been introduced to enable the student to read further textbooks if he so desires. The teacher should consider very carefully which symbols are appropriate for primary-school children. Students should discuss this among themselves.

Sets and Subsets

The idea of a set is a simple one. Everyone is familiar with the term "collection". The toys in a toy box, the contents of a wallet and the people at the football match are all collections. The term "set" is a little more precise than this. The teddy bear was in the toy box but at the moment it is not. There is therefore some doubt as to whether the teddy bear is in the collection or not. This kind of doubt must not arise if it is justifiable to refer to the collection as a set. A set is often referred to as a "well-defined" collection. Here the words "well defined" are used to mean that it is possible to tell precisely whether any particular element is a member or not. In order that the toys in the toy box may be called a set it should be stated which toy box and at which instant of time. Thus the toys in *that* toy box at *this* instant of time form a set. The teddy bear which at *this* instant of time is on the floor is not a member of the set. The car at the bottom of the box is a member, and so on. The people who were on all the trains standing in Euston Station, London, at noon on Friday,

13th October 1967 are members of a set. It would not, however, be strictly correct to refer to all the children who are now in this classroom and have blue eyes as a set. There may be a dispute as to whether John Brown's eyes are blue or bluey-green, i.e. there is a doubt as to whether he is a member of the set or not. In practice difficulties of this kind rarely occur in the primary school. The word "set" should be part of the natural vocabulary of the teacher. In the infant school she may refer to this set of beads or that set of shells and ask if there are more conkers in this set than in that. The child gradually abstracts the idea of a set in the same way that he abstracts the idea of redness after handling and talking about all kinds of red objects. The formal definition of "well-defined collection" should *not* be given. Subsets may be formed by taking some or all of the elements of the set and considering them together.

Recording: Set Notation

When recording it is usual to use capital letters for the names of sets and small letters to stand for the elements. When listing the elements it is also usual to put them in between two curly brackets called "braces".

Thus we could write:

$$A = \{4, 6, 8, 10\} \quad \text{and} \quad B = \{a, b, c\}.$$

These would be read as "A is the set of numbers 4, 6, 8 and 10, and B is the set whose members are a, b and c.

Note. A purist would argue that A is the set of *numerals* standing for the numbers 4, 6, 8 and 10 and not the numbers themselves which are abstract. In spite of stressing "purity of language" in Chapter 1 this fine distinction will not be made.

The symbol $\in$ is used for "is a member of" or "is an element of" and the symbol $\notin$ means "is not a member of". Thus we could write $4 \in A$ and $a \notin A$ which would be read as 4 is a member of the set A; a is not a member of the set A.

Question. Given that C = {John, Tom, Dick, Harry} and $D = \{3, 4, 5, 6, 7\}$ insert the correct symbol, $\notin$ or $\in$, in the following: (i) John .... C, (ii) Tom .... D, (iii) 4 .... D.

Answers. (i) John $\in C$ (i.e. John is an element of C),
(ii) Tom $\notin D$ (i.e. Tom is not a member of D),
(iii) $4 \in D$ (i.e. 4 is a member of D).

Set Builder Form

It is possible to define a set by listing all the elements. For example, in the above the sets C and D are well defined because all the elements have been listed and it is possible to say with certainty whether an element is in the set or not. However, sets are much more useful when it is possible to state a property which is satisfied by the members of the set and not satisfied by the non-members.

In fact sets are used to classify objects with a view to studying more carefully their properties. The set A could have been described as the set of even numbers greater than 2 and less than 12. The number $3 \notin A$ since 3 is not an even number. The number $14 \notin A$ for although it is an even number it is not less than 12. The only even numbers greater than 2 and less than 12 are 4, 6, 8 and 10, and so these are the only members of this set. When a set is described by stating a property in this way it is often useful to record it in a form known as the "set builder" form. In this form a letter is chosen to represent a typical member and the property which defines the set stated. It is recorded as:

$$A = \{x | x \text{ is an even number and } 2 < x < 12\}.$$

In words it is read as:

A is a set of elements x, where x is an even number, and x is greater than 2 and less than 12,

or as:

A is the set of members x such that x is an even number and where 2 is less than x and x is less than 12.

Using this form the set D of the previous paragraph could be written as:

$$D = \{a | 2 < a < 8 \text{ and } a \text{ is a natural number}\}.$$

Note.

1. The vertical line, |, is sometimes replaced by: .

2. A natural number is a counting number and so the set of natural numbers is an infinite set starting with 1, 2, 3, 4, etc., and continuing indefinitely.

3. Experiments with top-class Juniors showed that set builder form was not too difficult for them to understand and use.

Q. 1. List the members of the following sets:

(i) $\{b : 6 < b < 15 \text{ and } b \text{ is a multiple of } 3\}$,

(ii) $\{x \mid 7 \leqslant x \leqslant 13 \text{ and } x \text{ is a prime number}\}$.

(The symbol $\leqslant$ means "less than or equal to".)

2. Express in set builder form the following:

(i) $\{5, 7, 9, 11, 13\}$, (ii) $\{5, 10, 15, 20, 25\}$.

A. 1. (i) $\{9, 12\}$, (ii) $\{7, 11, 13\}$.

2. (i) $\{a \mid 3 < a < 15 \text{ and } a \text{ is an odd number}\}$,

(ii) $\{b \mid b < 30 \text{ and } b \text{ is a multiple of } 5\}$.

Empty Set

Consider the following set:

$$\{x : 2 < x < 4 \text{ and } x \text{ is an even number}\}.$$

There are no even numbers between 2 and 4 and so the set has no members. There was a property stated but no elements satisfied the property. It is a set containing no elements and is called the *empty set*. It is often denoted by { } or Ø. It is sometimes also called the null set. Note that {0} is not an empty set. It is a set which contains one member, namely zero.

Other examples of the empty set are:

(a) The set of people who were on Euston Station, London, at noon on Friday, 13th October 1966.
(Note that 13th October 1966 was not a Friday.)

(b) The set of negative numbers greater than 2.

Q. Which of the following sets are empty?

(i) $\{a : a \text{ is an equilateral right-angled triangle}\}$,

(ii) $\{b : 3 < b < 5 \text{ and } b \text{ is an odd number}\}$,

(iii) $\{c : -1 < c < 1 \text{ and } c \text{ is an integer}\}$.

A. (i) and (ii) are empty sets; (iii) is not an empty set for it contains one member, namely 0.

Subsets

Consider the sets C and D where

$$C = \{3, 6, 9, 12\} \quad \text{and} \quad D = \{6, 9\}.$$

Here all the members of set D are also members of set C. We say that D is a subset of C. Since there are some members of C which are not members of D we could also say that D is a *proper* subset of C. The empty set and the set itself are both regarded as subsets but they are not *proper subsets*. The following examples will help to clarify this.

(i) Given that $A = \{a, b, c\}$ list all the subsets of A.
The subsets are: $\{a, b, c\}$, $\{a, b\}$, $\{a, c\}$, $\{b, c\}$, $\{a\}$, $\{b\}$, $\{c\}$, $\{\ \}$.

Note. There are eight subsets in all when the original set contains three members. There are sixteen subsets when it contains four members. Can you spot the pattern? Why is there this pattern?

(ii) Given that $A = \{a, b, c\}$ list all the *proper subsets* of A.
The proper subsets are: $\{a, b\}$, $\{a, c\}$, $\{b, c\}$, $\{a\}$, $\{b\}$, $\{c\}$.

Note. The set $\{b, a\}$ is regarded as the same as the set $\{a, b\}$, i.e. the order of the elements is immaterial.

The symbol used to denote D "is a proper subset of" C is $\subset$.

Thus we write $D \subset C$ and say that this means D is a proper subset of C or that D is included in C.

The symbol for "is a subset of" is $\subseteq$. This symbol allows for the possibility that the subset is also the set itself. (Compare the symbols $\subset$ and

$\subseteq$ for sets with the symbols $<$ and $\leqslant$ which mean "less than" and "less than or equal to", respectively.)

Q. 1. Given that $P = \{x \mid 2 < x < 8$ and x is a natural number$\}$

and $Q = \{y \mid 2 < y\ 8$ and y is an even number$\}$,

is it true that $Q \subset P$?

2. Given that $R = \{a \mid a$ is any isosceles triangle$\}$

and $S = \{b \mid b$ is any equilateral triangle$\}$,

is it true that $R \subset S$?

A. 1. Yes. The members of P are 3, 4, 5, 6, 7 and the members of Q are 4 and 6. Thus all the members of Q are members of P and there are some members of P which are not members of Q.

2. No. An equilateral triangle is isosceles but an isosceles triangle need not be equilateral. It is true therefore that $S \subset R$ not that $R \subset S$.

Universal Set

When we are considering several different subsets of a given set it is often convenient to refer to this original set as the *universal set*. In other words, the universal set is the set under consideration at any particular time. In a classroom situation it might be convenient to refer to all the children in the class as the universal set. Subsets of this could be the set of children in the room who were wearing glasses, or the set of all the children in the room who were wearing black shoes, or the set of children in the room who were over 30 years of age. It is probable that this latter is the empty set!

Q. Given that the universal set is the set of natural numbers less than twenty, list the members of the following subsets:

(i) $\{a : a$ is a multiple of $2\}$,

(ii) $\{b : b$ is a multiple of $4\}$,

(iii) $\{c : c$ is a prime number greater than $19\}$.

A. (i) $\{2, 4, 6, 8, 10, 12, 14, 16, 18\}$,

(ii) $\{4, 8, 12, 16\}$,

(iii) $\{\,\}$ since there are no prime numbers greater than 19 and less than 20.

Note. Since the universal set had been clearly stated for all these subsets it was not necessary, for example, to write (i) as $\{a : a \text{ is a multiple of 2 and } a \text{ is a natural number less than } 20\}$.

Union and Intersection of Two Sets

Let $X = \{2, 4, 6, 8, 10, 12\}$ and $Y = \{3, 6, 9, 12\}$. The set consisting of all those members which are members of either X or Y or both is called the *union* of X and Y. It is denoted by: $X \cup Y$.

Thus $X \cup Y = \{2, 3, 4, 6, 8, 9, 10, 12\}$. It is not usual to repeat members which are common to both sets.

The set consisting of all those members which are elements of *both* X and Y is called the *intersection* of the two sets. It is denoted by $X \cap Y$. Thus $X \cap Y = \{6, 12\}$.

Q. 1. Given that $A = \{a, b, c, d, e\}$, $B = \{a, c, e, g\}$ and $C = \{f, g\}$, find (i) $A \cup B$, (ii) $A \cap B$, (iii) $B \cap C$, (iv) $(A \cap B) \cap C$.
Do you think that the brackets are needed in (iv)?

2. Given that D is the set of all right-angled triangles and E is the set of all isosceles triangles, explain what $D \cap E$ represents.

3. The universal set for the following subsets is: $\{1, 2, 3, 4, 5, 6, 7, 8, 9\}$.
$F = \{x : x \text{ is even}\}$, $G = \{y : y \text{ is exactly divisible by } 3\}$, $H = \{z : z \text{ is a prime number}\}$.
Find (i) $F \cup G$, (ii) $(F \cap G) \cap H$.

A. 1. (i) $A \cup B = \{a, b, c, d, e, g\}$, (ii) $A \cap B = \{a, c, e\}$, (iii) $B \cap C = \{g\}$, (iv) $\{\,\}$.
The brackets are not needed since $(A \cap B) \cap C = A \cap (B \cap C)$.

2. $D \cap E$ is the set of all right-angled isosceles triangles.

3. (i) $F \cup G = \{2, 3, 4, 6, 8, 9\}$, (ii) $(F \cap G) \cap H = \{\,\}$ since $F \cap G = \{6\}$ and 6 is not a prime number.

The idea of union and intersection can easily be extended to more than two sets as these examples show. Brackets are not needed since union and intersection both obey the associative laws.

Disjoint Sets

When two sets have no members in common the intersection is obviously the empty set. The sets are then said to be *disjoint*.

Clearly the sets $\{a, b, c, d\}$ and $\{e, f, g\}$ have no members in common and so they are disjoint. The set of all equilateral triangles and the set of all right-angled triangles are disjoint sets.

Question. Are the set of all prime numbers and the set of all even numbers disjoint?

Answer. No. 2 is a prime and it is even. It is in fact the only even prime number.

Cardinal Number of a Set

It is important not to confuse the elements of a set with the number of elements of a set.

In the previous example the set $X = \{2, 4, 6, 8, 10, 12\}$ had six members and the set $Y = \{3, 6, 9, 12\}$ had four members. We say that the cardinal number of X is six and of Y is four. This is recorded as $n(X) = 6$ and $n(Y) = 4$.

The union of X and Y, i.e. $X \cup Y$, does not contain ten members $(6+4)$ but only eight. This is because X and Y are *not disjoint* sets but have members in common. It is only when disjoint sets are united that the cardinal number of the union is the sum of the cardinal numbers of the separate sets.

Thus, $n(A \cup B) = n(A)+n(B)$ *if and only if* A and B are disjoint sets.

Q. For which of the following pairs of sets A and B is it true that $n(A)+n(B) = n(A \cup B)$?

(i) $A = \{a : a < 10 \text{ and } a \text{ is an even number}\}$,

$B = \{b : b < 12 \text{ and } b \text{ is divisible by three}\}$,

(ii) $A = \{a : a < 10 \text{ and } a \text{ is an even number}\}$,

$B = \{b : b < 11 \text{ and } b \text{ is an odd number}\}$.

A. It is false for (i) since $A \cap B = 6$. It is true for (ii) since A and B have no members in common, i.e.

$$A \cap B = \emptyset.$$

Partition of a Set

Consider the example:

Let U be the universal set of all the children in the class.

Let B be the subset of all the boys and G the subset of all the girls. Clearly B and G cannot have any members in common. They are disjoint sets. Also the union of B and G is the universal set since a child must be either a boy or a girl.

In symbols: $B \cap G = \emptyset$ and $B \cup G = U$.

U is said to be *partitioned* into two subsets B and G. The idea of partitioning can be extended to the case where there are more than two subsets. The following example illustrates this.

A bag contains beads some of which are coloured red, some yellow and the rest white. Let U be the universal set of all the beads in the bag, R the set of all the red beads, Y the set of all the yellow beads and W the set of all the white beads.

Clearly (i) $R \cup Y \cup W = U$, (ii) $R \cap Y = \emptyset$, (ii) $Y \cap W = \emptyset$ and (iv) $R \cap W = \emptyset$. In words this means that no bead can be in more than one subset and the union of all the three subsets is the universal set. Thus the universal set, U, has been *partitioned.*

A universal set has been partitioned if and only if (i) the union of all the subsets is the universal set and (ii) all the subsets taken in pairs have no members in common. The idea of partitioning a set is particularly important in Infant and Junior schools. If a set containing five toys is partitioned into two subsets it is possible to discover that $3+2 = 5$ and that $2+3 = 5$. A different partition might show that $1+4 = 5$ and that $4+1 = 5$. Partitioning sets in different ways enables children to discover number relationships.

Q. 1. Given that $U = \{1, 2, 3, 4, 5, 6, 7\}$, $A = \{1, 3, 5\}$, $B = \{2, 4\}$, and $C = \{7\}$, has the set U been partitioned?

2. Given that $U = \{1, 2, 3, 4, 5, 6, 7\}$, $A = \{1, 3, 5, 7\}$, $B = \{2, 4\}$ and $C = \{6, 7\}$, has the set U been partitioned?

3. Given that $U = \{1, 2, 3, 4, 5, 6, 7\}$, $A = \{1, 3, 5\}$, $B = \{2, 4, 6\}$ and $C = \{7\}$, has the set U been partitioned?

A. 1. No, since 6 does not appear in any subset and thus the union of A, B and C is not the universal set.

2. No, since A and C are not disjoint sets. They have the member 7 in common, i.e. $A \cap C = \{7\}$.

3. Yes, since the union of the three subsets is the universal set and the three subsets taken in pairs are disjoint.

Venn Diagrams

It is sometimes helpful to draw a diagram to represent a set. Consider the universal set, U, and subsets X and Y where $U = \{1, 2, 3, 4, 5, 6, 7, 8, 9, 10, 11, 12\}$, $X = \{2, 4, 6, 8, 10, 12\}$ and $Y = \{3, 6, 9, 12\}$.

A closed curve is drawn and points inside the region are chosen to represent the members of the set.

Thus if X is represented by:

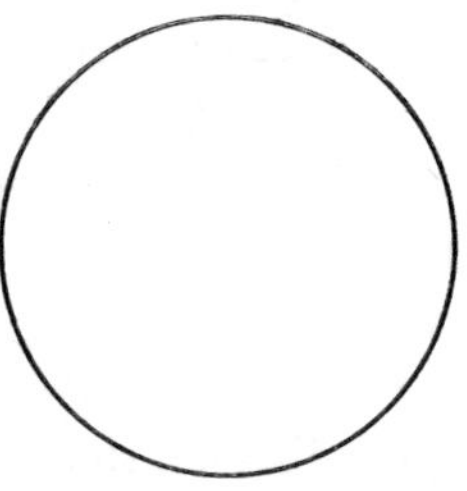

then the elements 2, 4, 6, 8, 10 and 12 will be represented by points inside the closed region.

If another circle is drawn to represent Y it must intersect the first circle since elements 6 and 12 belong to both sets X and Y.

The diagram could look something like:

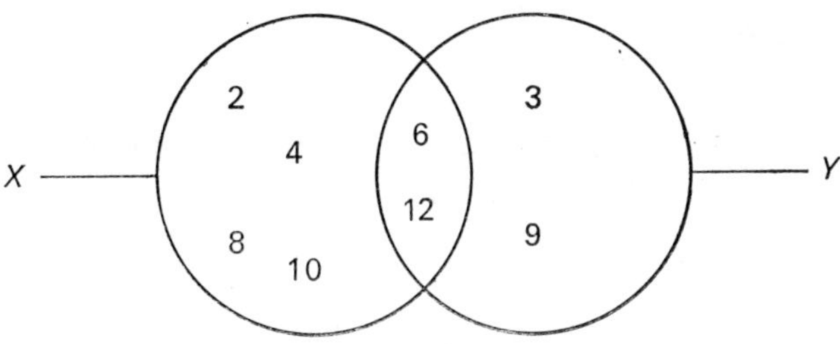

Such a diagram is called a Venn diagram.

In such a Venn diagram the intersection of the two sets, $X \cap Y$, is represented by the shaded region:

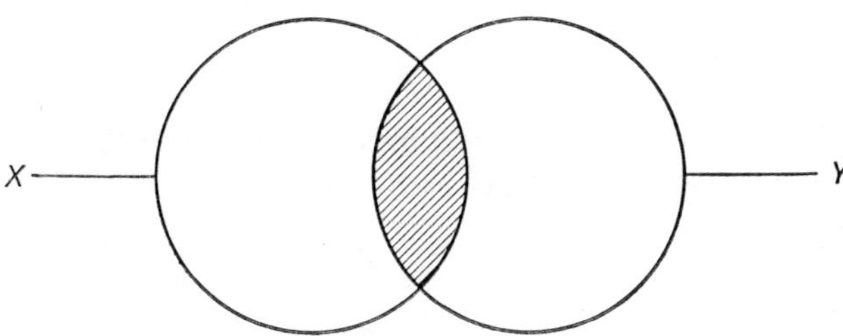

The union of X and Y, $X \cup Y$ is represented by the following shaded region:

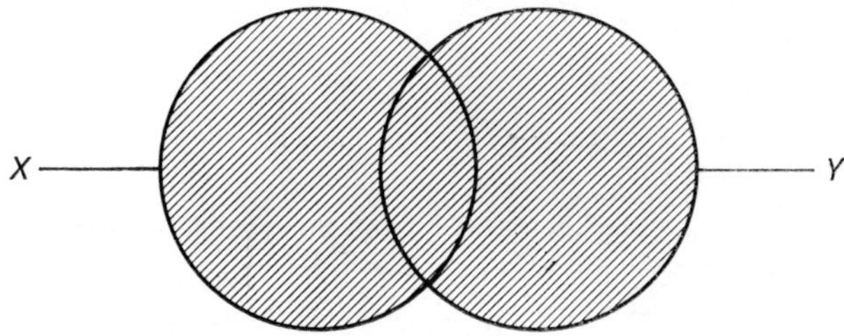

The universal set is often denoted by a rectangle and so the sets U, X and Y together with their elements could be shown thus:

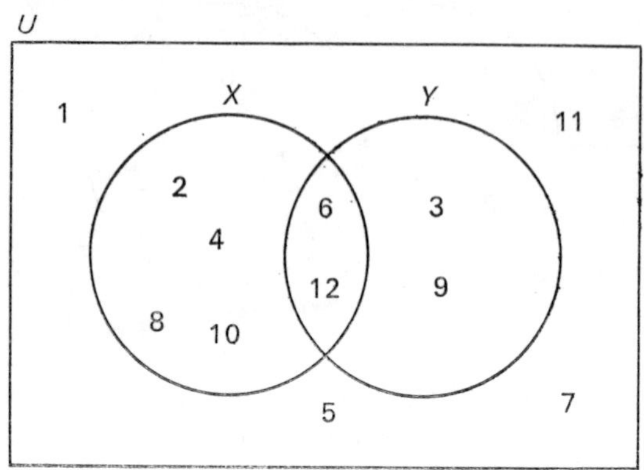

Complement of a Set

In the previous example consider the subset of U which contains all the members which are not members of X. This set is called the complement of X and is denoted by X'. It is sometimes referred to as "not X", i.e. the elements which are in U but not in X.

Thus $X' = \{1, 3, 5, 7, 9, 11\}$.

In a Venn diagram the complement would be the shaded region as shown:

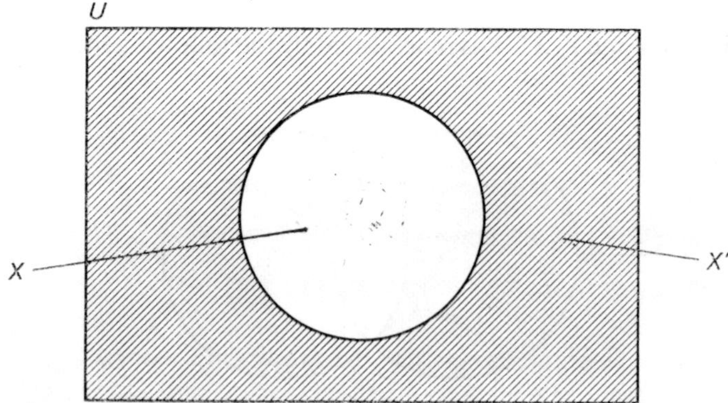

Q. Show the following sets in a Venn diagram:

$$U = \{x \mid x \leqslant 15 \text{ and } x \text{ is a natural number}\},$$

$$A = \{y \mid y \leqslant 15 \text{ and } y \text{ is an even number}\}$$

and $$B = \{z \mid z \leqslant 15 \text{ and } z \text{ is divisible by } 3\}.$$

A. 

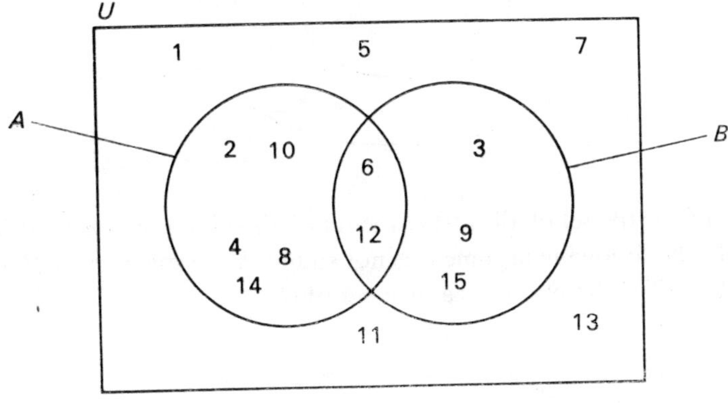

Venn Diagrams to illustrate Logical Arguments

Venn diagrams are particularly useful when illustrating the soundness or otherwise of a logical argument. The following examples illustrate:

1. Let G be the set of all cats, H the set of all animals and g represent a particular cat. Clearly G is a subset of H. The following argument can be put forward:

g is a member of G (in symbols $g \in G$).

G is a subset of H (in symbols $G \subset H$).

Therefore g is a member of H (in symbols $\rightarrow g \in H$).

In other words, g is a cat and all cats are animals therefore g is an animal.

The Venn diagram shows that the argument is sound, for since G is a subset of H the region denoting G must lie completely inside the region denoting H. The member g is inside the inner region and is therefore clearly in H:

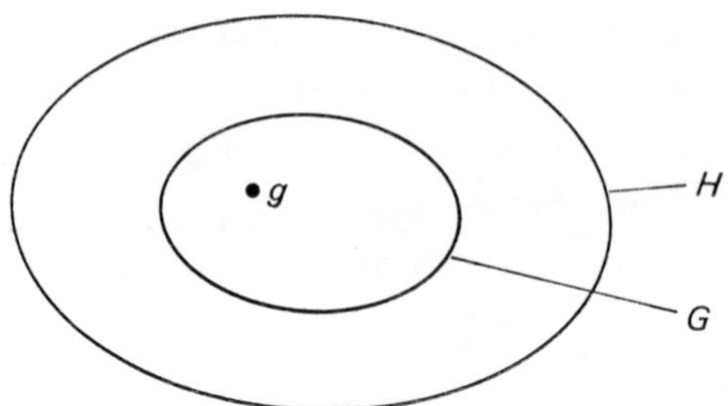

2. Let G be the set of all cats, H the set of all animals and h a particular animal. The following argument is not sound. h is a member of H and G is a subset of H therefore h is a member of G:

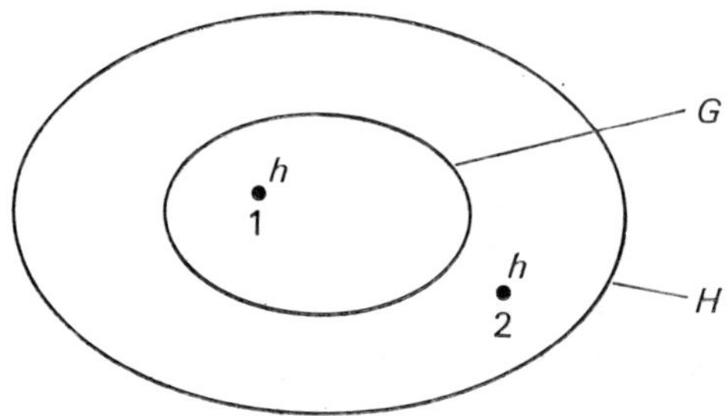

The Venn diagram shows clearly that the argument is not sound because it could be in either of the two positions as shown by the figures 1 and 2.

It is important to note that the Venn diagram illustrates that the argument is not sound: it does not state whether the conclusion is correct or not. It is quite possible to get a true statement following an unsound argument.

Revision Exercises

Questions:

1. U, X and Y are the sets as stated previously in the text.
Express U, X and Y in set builder form.

2. List the elements of the sets P, Q, P', Q', $P \cap Q$, $P \cup Q$, $(P \cap Q)'$, and $(P \cup Q)'$ where

$U = \{a \mid a$ is a natural number and $a \leqslant 10\}$,

$P = \{b \mid b$ is an odd natural number and $b \leqslant 9\}$,

$Q = \{c \mid c$ is five times a natural number and $c \leqslant 10\}$.

Show also the elements of P, Q and U in a Venn diagram.

(*Note.* The natural numbers are sometimes called the counting numbers.)

3. Give an example of an empty set. Ask your friend or tutor to check your solution.

4. Shade regions in appropriate Venn diagrams to show that

$$A \cup (B \cap C) = (A \cup B) \cap (A \cup C).$$

5. Given that A is the set of natural numbers less than 50 which are multiples of 18, B is the set of natural numbers less than 50 which are multiples of 6 and C is the set of natural numbers less than 50 which are multiples of 8, list the elements of the set $(A \cup B) \cap (A \cup C)$.
Use question 4 to help you to check your result.

6. Make some examples up for yourselves.

Answers:

1. $U = \{u \mid u$ is a natural number and $u \leqslant 12\}$.

$X = \{x \mid x \in U$ and x is even$\}$.

$Y = \{y \mid y \in U$ and y is a multiple of three$\}$.

Note. There are several other ways of expressing the results.

2. $P = \{1, 3, 5, 7, 9\}$.

$Q = \{5, 10\}$.

$P' = \{2, 4, 6, 8, 10\}$.

$Q' = \{1, 2, 3, 4, 6, 7, 8, 9\}$.

$P \cap Q = \{5\}$.

$P \cup Q = \{1, 3, 5, 7, 9, 10\}$.

$(P \cap Q)' = \{1, 2, 3, 4, 6, 7, 8, 9, 10\}$.

$(P \cup Q)' = \{2, 4, 6, 8\}$.

2. (*cont.*)

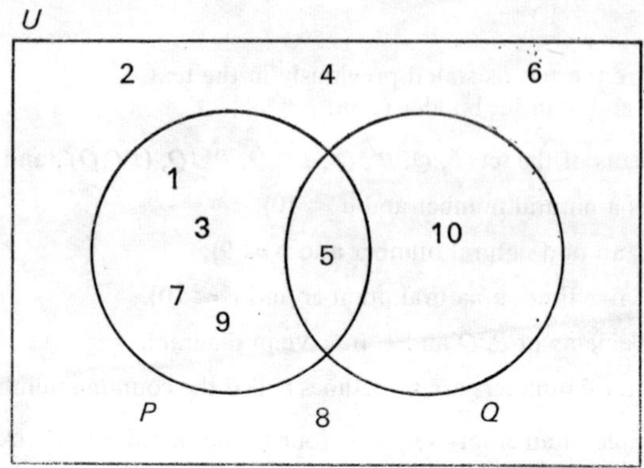

4.

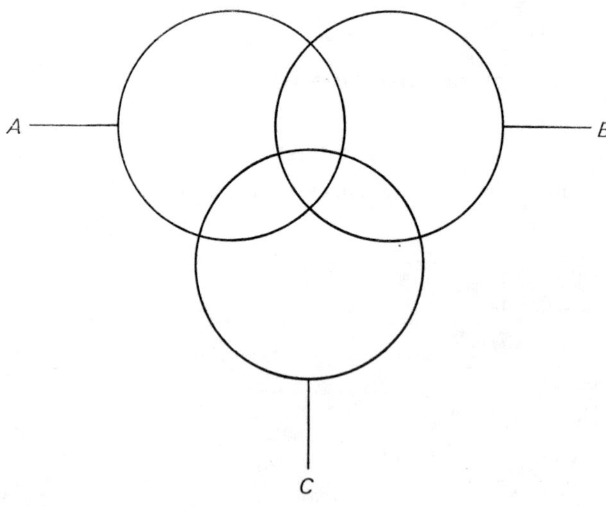

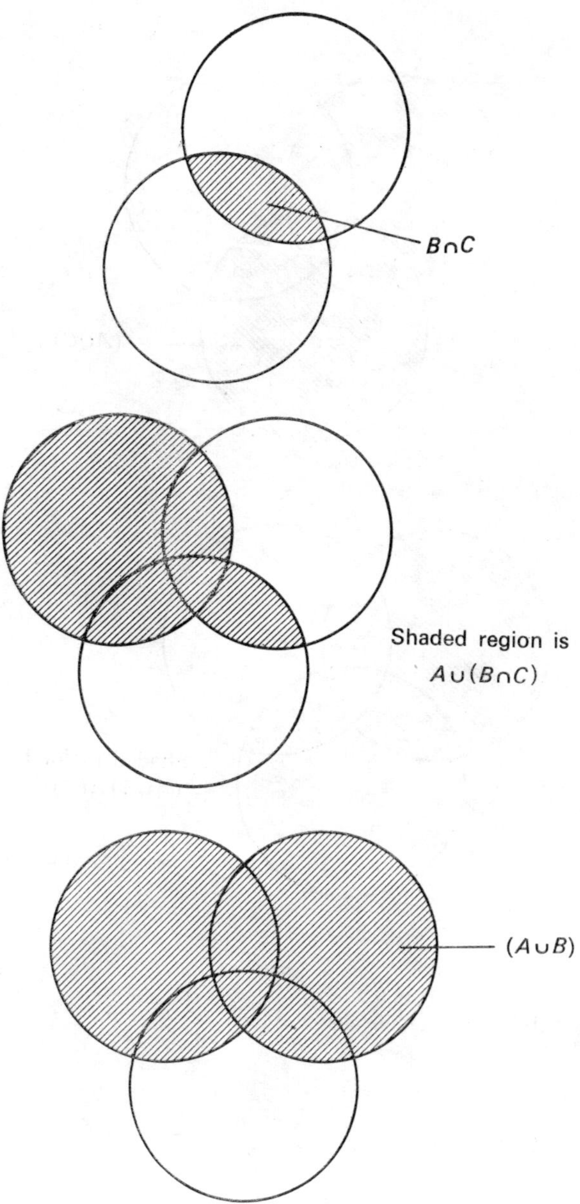
B∩C
Shaded region is
A∪(B∩C)
(A∪B)

4. (*cont.*)

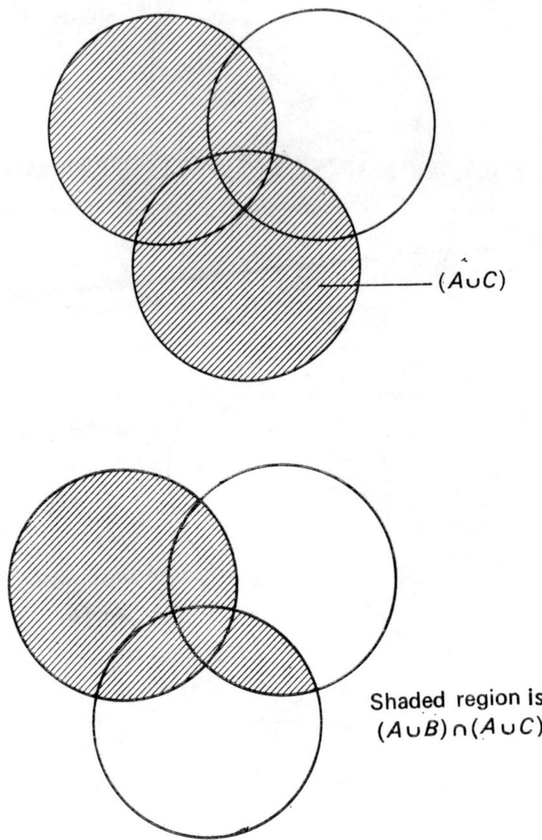

5. $(A \cup B) \cap (A \cup C) = \{18, 24, 36, 48\}$.

CHAPTER 3

RELATIONS AND SORTING

A SET of four boys, Edward, Fred, George and Harry were asked to say which drinks they liked out of the following list: Coffee, Lemonade, Milk, Tea and Water. Their replies were recorded thus:

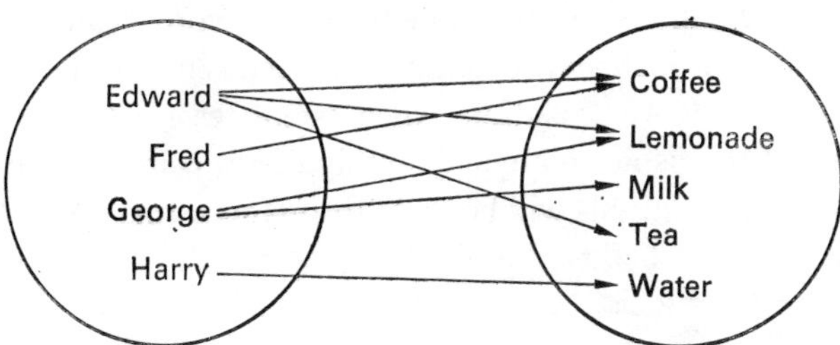

Relation: "likes to drink"

The arrows indicate, for instance, that Edward likes to drink Coffee, Lemonade and Tea.

The facts could also have been listed thus:

{(Edward, Coffee), (Edward, Lemonade), (Edward, Tea), (Fred, Coffee), (George, Lemonade), (George, Milk), (Harry, Water)}.

We say that there is a *relation* between the set of boys and the set of drinks. Here the relation is "likes to drink". (Edward, Coffee) is called an *ordered pair*. The order is important for if we wrote (Coffee, Edward) with the same relation it would mean that coffee likes to drink Edward. The first member of the ordered pair, usually called the first coordinate, must be a member of the set *from which* the arrows are drawn and the second member of the pair, called the second coordinate, must be a member of the set *to which* the arrows are drawn. The members of the second set are referred to as images. Thus, Edward has three images, namely coffee, lemonade and tea whilst Fred has only one image, coffee. This relation is called a *many-many relation* since there are members of the first set which have more than one image and there are members of the second set which are the images of more than one first coordinate.

The word *relation* has been used here in two different senses:

(i) it has been used to describe the abstract idea which picks out a set of ordered pairs, and
(ii) it has also been used as the name of the set of ordered pairs.

This is not universally accepted. Sometimes the word "rule" is used to describe the abstract idea and sometimes the idea is put in the form of an open sentence the word "relation" then being reserved for the set of ordered pairs. There is not really any ambiguity in using the word "relation" in two senses and this will be done throughout this book. It will be clear in the context whether the word is used for the subset of ordered pairs or the abstract idea.

Cartesian Product

In the previous example we had two sets, namely, a set, S, of boys, names and a set, T, of names of drinks.

S = {Edward, Fred, George, Harry}

and T = {Coffee, Lemonade, Milk, Tea, Water}.

Consider now the set of all possible ordered pairs where the first coordinate is a member of S and the second coordinate is a member of T. This set is called the Cartesian Cross Product or the Cartesian Product of S and T. It is denoted by $S \times T$. Thus $S \times T$ = {(Edward, Coffee), (Edward, Lemonade), (Edward, Milk), (Edward, Tea), (Edward, Water), (Fred, Coffee), (Fred, Lemonade), . . . (Harry, Water)}.

There are four members of the set S and five members of the set T and so there are twenty members of the Cartesian Product, $S \times T$.

Note that the relation, {(Edward, Coffee), (Edward, Lemonade), (Edward, Tea), (Fred, Coffee), (George, Lemonade), (George, Milk), (Harry, Water)} is a subset of $S \times T$. Hence a relation can be defined as a subset of a Cartesian Product.

Remembering that the word "relation" may be used in two senses, it is possible to regard the relation as either the subset of the Cartesian Product or the abstract idea that produces the subset.

The Cartesian Product is sometimes called the direct product. It may be expressed in set builder form as:

$$S \times T = \{(x,y) : x \in S \text{ and } y \in T\}.$$

This is read as:

The Cartesian Product, $S \times T$, is the set of all ordered pairs, (x, y), such that x is a member of S and y is a member of T.

The above relation can also be expressed in set builder form as:

$$R = \{(x, y) : x \in S,\ y \in T \text{ and } x \text{ likes to drink } y\}.$$

This is read as:

The relation, R, is the set of all ordered pairs, (x, y), such that x is a member of S, y is a member of T and x likes to drink y.

The phrase "x likes to drink y" is an open sentence which is either true or false for every member of the Cartesian Product, $S \times T$. The relation is then the set of all the ordered pairs for which this open sentence is true. A relation is therefore sometimes referred to as a truth set.

(*Note.* Open Sentences and Truth Sets are considered in more detail in Chapter 5.)

Q. 1. Given that $P = \{a, b, c\}$ and $Q = \{v, w\}$

(i) express $P \times Q$ and $Q \times P$ in set builder form and
(ii) list all the members of $P \times Q$ and $Q \times P$.

2. Given that $S = \{1, 2, 3\}$ and $T = \{1, 2, 3, 4, 5, 6\}$ list the members of the relation, R, where $R = \{(x, y) : x \in S, y \in T \text{ and } y = 2x\}$. Show this relation on a diagram with arrows going from the members of S to their appropriate images in T.

A. 1. $P \times Q = \{(x, y) : x \in P \text{ and } y \in Q\}$.

$Q \times P = \{(x, y) : x \in Q \text{ and } y \in P\}$.

$P \times Q = \{a, v), (a, w), (b, v), (b, w), (c, v), (c, w)\}$.

$Q \times P = \{v, a), (v, b), (v, c), (w, a), (w, b), (w, c)\}$.

2. $R = \{(1, 2), (2, 4), (3, 6)\}$.

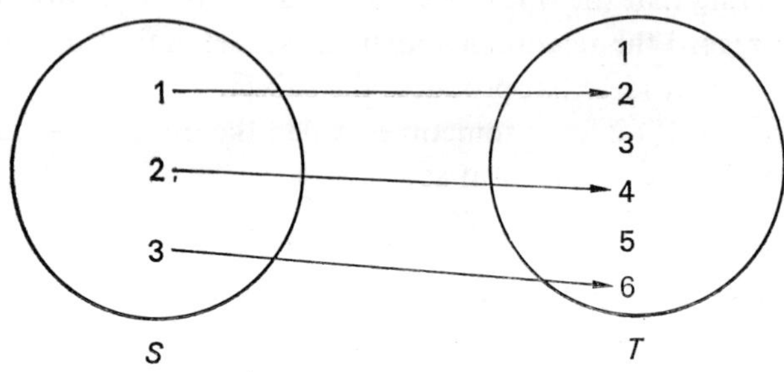

Let us consider the question 2 above further. The set, S, is called the *domain* of the relation. The subset of T which consists only of those members which are images is called the *range* of the relation. Thus in question 2 the domain is $\{1, 2, 3\}$ and the range is $\{2, 4, 6\}$.

Note. The domain need not be the set S but is a subset of S whilst the range is a subset of T.

Q. The following diagram shows a relation. State the domain and the range.

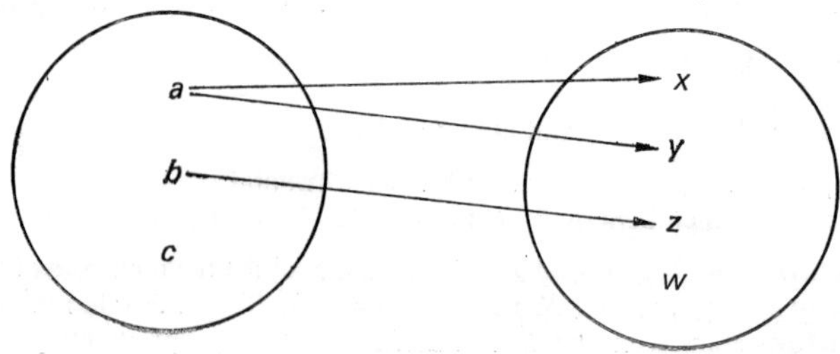

A. The domain = $\{a, b\}$ and the range = $\{x, y, z\}$.
(Note that c is not in the domain since it has no image and w is not in the range since it is not the image of any member.)

Mapping

Alice, Brenda and Charles respectively own a doll, ball and a bat.

Let A = {Alice, Brenda, Charles} and

B = {Doll, Ball, Bat}.

The Cartesian Product, $A \times B$ = {(Alice, Doll), (Alice, Ball), (Alice, Bat), (Brenda, Doll), (Brenda, Ball), (Brenda, Bat), (Charles, Doll), (Charles, Ball), (Charles, Bat)}.

Consider the relation, R, where $R = \{(x, y) : x \in A, y \in B$ and x owns $y\}$.

It may be represented diagramatically thus:

"Owns"

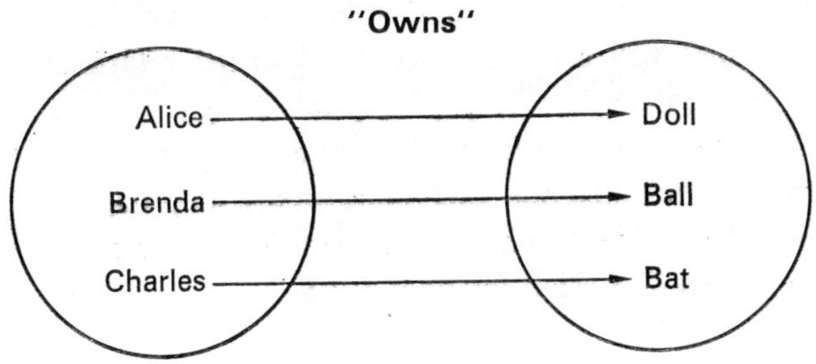

Every member of the first set has one and only one image. This kind of relation is called a *mapping*. In this case the mapping is a one-to-one mapping. It is possible for the mapping to be many to one as the next example illustrates.

Example. Edward, Fred, George and Harry were asked to choose which drink they liked best out of Coffee, Lemonade, Tea, Milk and Water. Each one of them had to choose *one and only one* drink. Their choices are shown in the diagram:

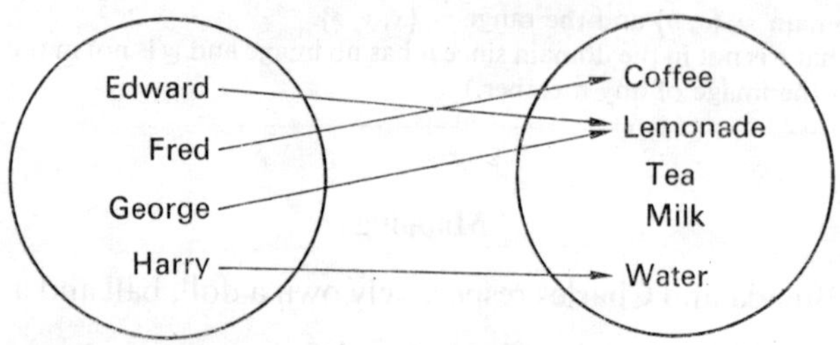

Edward and George both chose Lemonade, i.e. Lemonade is the image of more than one member. This relation is called a many-to-one relation. It is still a mapping since every member of the first set has exactly one image. It is called a many-to-one mapping because there are some elements of the second set which are the images of more than one element of the first set—hence the word "many", but the elements of the first set have only one image—hence the word "one".

Some books describe all relations as mappings and speak of "many-to-many mappings". This is not desirable and throughout this book the word "mapping" will only be used to describe relations where *every* member of the first set has *one and only one image*.

To summarize, a many–many and a one–many relations are not mappings. A many–one and a one–one relations are mappings.

When all the elements under consideration belong to one set, it is possible to have a Cartesian Product $S \times S$.

Example. $S = \{1, 2, 3, 4\}$ and $R = \{(x, y) : x \in S,\ y \in S \text{ and } y > x\}$. Expressing $S \times S$ and R in list form we have:

$$S \times S = \{(1, 1), (1, 2), (1, 3), (1, 4), (2, 1), (2, 2), (2, 3), (2, 4), (3, 1), (3, 2), (3, 3), (3, 4), (4, 1), (4, 2), (4, 3), (4, 4)\},$$

and $$R = \{(1, 2), (1, 3), (1, 4), (2, 3), (2, 4), (3, 4)\}.$$

The relation could also be shown on a diagram thus:

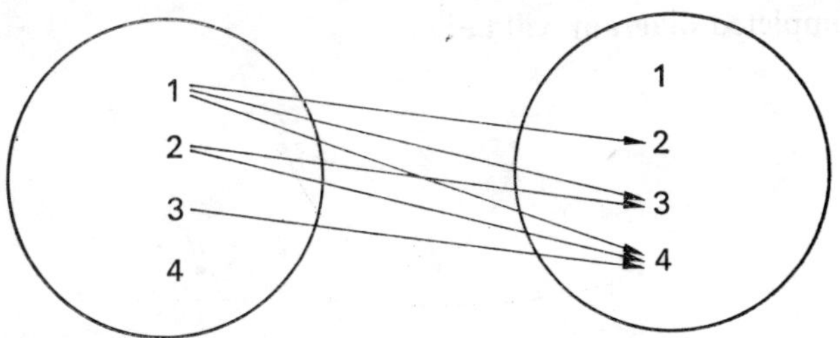

This is a many-to-many relation and is not a mapping.

Algebraic relations of this kind are important and will be considered more fully in Book 2.

Another way of representing relations when only one set is involved is illustrated by the following example.

Mr. and Mrs. Brown have three children, Alice, Bernard and Clifford. Mr. and Mrs. Smith have three children, David, Elizabeth and Freda.

Consider the set consisting of the six children denoting them by the initial letters of their christian names, i.e. $S = \{a, b, c, d, e, f\}$, where a represents Alice, b represents Bernard and so on.

The members of S can be represented by six points thus:

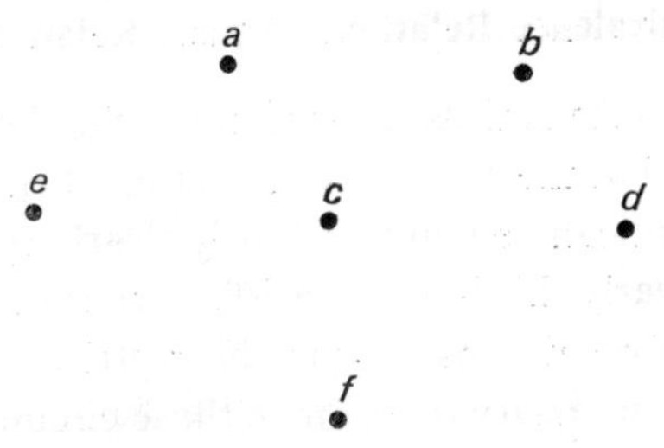

Now consider the relation "is the brother of". This may be indicated in the diagram by drawing an arrow from b to a signifying that b is the brother of a. Since b and c are both male there will not only be an arrow from b to c but also one from c to b.

The completed diagram will be:

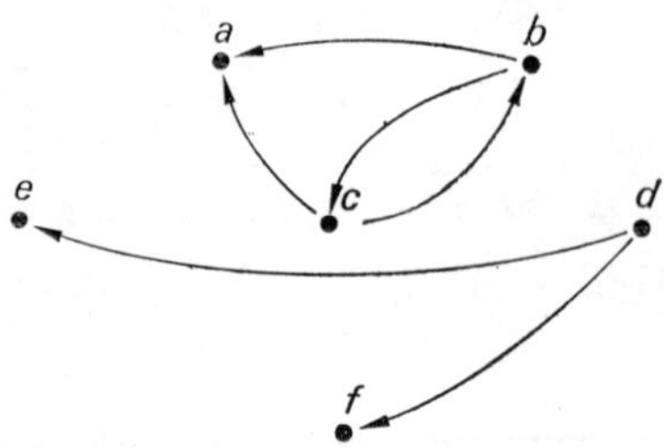

The relation is a subset of $S \times S$ and, in set builder form, can be expressed as

$$R = \{(x.y) \mid x \in S,\ y \in S \text{ and } y \text{ is the brother of } x\}.$$

As an exercise list the members of R. The solution is given:

$$R = \{(a, b), (a, c), (b, c), (c, b), (e, d), (f, d)\}.$$

It should therefore be noted that a relation can either be shown using a diagram or expressed in set builder form or expressed as a list.

Equivalence Relations (Equals Relations)

The word equal is often misused in primary school mathematics. Originally it is probable that the word was only used when things were identically equal. 5 is identically equal to 5 but is clearly not identically equal to $3+2$ or $8-3$. Clearly this is an unsatisfactory restriction of the meaning of the word. Before dispensing with this restriction and widening the use of the word it is necessary to examine those circumstances where it is felt justifiable to use the term. Upon analysis three properties emerge which are necessary before things may be considered to be equal in some way.

The first property seems almost too obvious to need stating. It is simply that something must be equal to itself, i.e. a must always be equal to a.

The second property is that if a is equal to b then b must be equal to a.

The third property is that if a is equal to b and b is equal to c then a must be equal to c.

These three are known as the *reflexive*, *symmetric* and *transitive* properties, respectively. If a relation is such that these three properties are all satisfied then it is called an *equivalence relation*. Under these circumstances it is justifiable to use the sign for equals, namely $=$.

The following examples serve to illustrate.

1. The relation "is the same shape" is an equivalence relation for

(i) a shape, x, clearly has the same shape as itself,

(ii) if x has the same shape as y then clearly y has the same shape as x and

(iii) if x has the same shape as y and y has the same shape as z then clearly x has the same shape as z.

2. The relation "has the same colour" is an equivalence relation for

(i) p has the same colour as p (reflexive property),

(ii) if p has the same colour as q, then q has the same colour as p (symmetric property) and

(iii) if p has the same colour as q, and q has the same colour as r then p has the same colour as r (transitive property).

3. The relation "weighs within $\frac{1}{2}$ kilogram" is *not* an equivalence relation.

Let a weigh 6 kilograms, b weigh $6\frac{3}{8}$ kilograms and c weigh $6\frac{3}{4}$ kilograms.

(i) The reflexive property is satisfied since a clearly weighs within $\frac{1}{2}$ kilogram of a and similarly for b and c.

(ii) The symmetric property is satisfied since if a weighs within $\frac{1}{2}$ kilogram of b then b weighs within $\frac{1}{2}$ kilogram of a.

(iii) The transitive property is *not* satisfied. Clearly a weighs within $\frac{1}{2}$ kilogram of b and b weighs within $\frac{1}{2}$ kilogram of c but a does not weigh within $\frac{1}{2}$ kilogram of c.

In the same way "is approximately equal" is not an equivalence relation. The reader may perhaps remember that if one uses four-figure logarithmic tables to evaluate 2×3 the result is 5·999. It is *not* correct to write

$$2 \times 3 = 5{\cdot}999.$$

The correct symbol to be used in this case is $\triangleq$ which means "is approximately equal".

Whenever the sign "=" is used the reader must know which relation is being considered at the time and must also be satisfied that it is an equivalence relation.

4. The relation "*is another way of writing*" is an important equivalence relation.

The cardinal number of a set is an abstract property of a set which is dealt with more fully later in the chapter. It will suffice at this stage to say that the "fiveness" of a set containing five objects is recorded using the *numeral* 5. If the Roman system of recording is used the numeral would be V. Thus 5, V, $(3+2)$, $(15 \div 3)$ are all ways of writing five. The reader can easily show that the three tests for an equivalence relation are satisfied for this relation.

It is therefore suggested that when the statement

$$3+2 = 5$$

is recorded in the primary school it is preferable to read this as 3 plus 2 is another way of writing 5 rather than

3 plus 2 equals 5.

Equivalence Classes

Consider a set, W, which consists of three square shapes, s_1, s_2, s_3 and two circular shapes c_1 and c_2 as shown at top of next page.

Consider further the relation "has the same shape". Clearly s_1, s_2 and s_3 will be in one subset and c_1 and c_2 will be in another subset. W has been partitioned by the relation. If we wish to see an example of a square shape any of s_1, s_2 or s_3 would do and similarly if we wish to see an example of a circular shape either c_1 or c_2 would do. We say that the equivalence

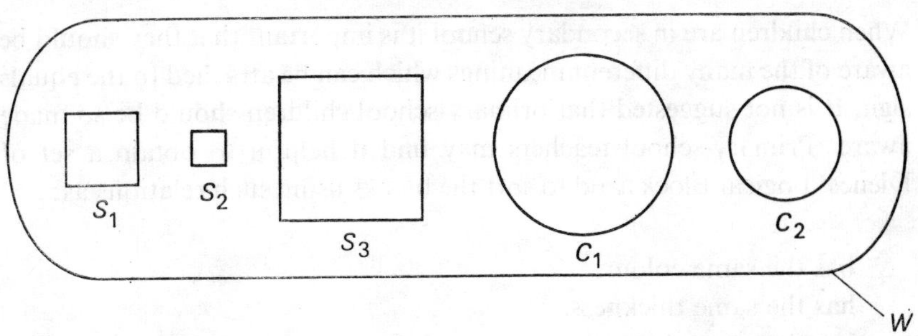

relation has partitioned the set into equivalence classes. Any member of a particular class is representative of all the members of the class.

The diagram shows the partition:

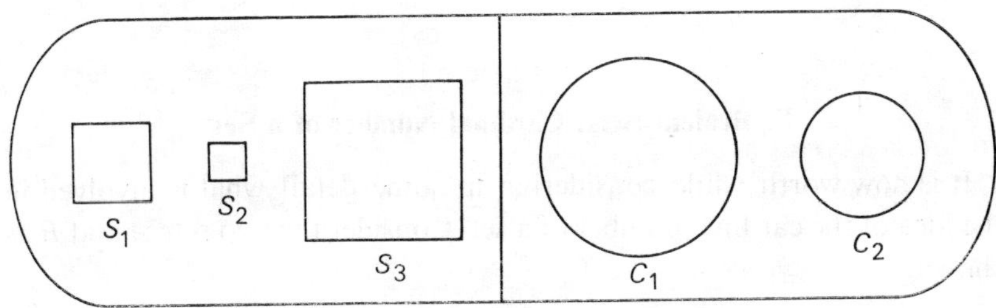

Whenever the "equals" sign, =, is used the assertion is being made that the two elements which are said to be equal are both members of the same equivalence class into which the universal set has been partitioned.

In secondary-school geometry one may find the statement

$$\text{triangle } ABC = \text{triangle } XYZ.$$

This is ambiguous until the precise equivalence relation is known.

If the relation is "has the same area" then all that is being asserted is that the triangles both have the same area. If, on the other hand, the relation is "has the same shape" it is probable that the triangles are similar though if the word "shape" is used in its widest sense the statement may mean no more than simply stating that the triangles are both triangles.

When children are in secondary school it is important that they should be aware of the many different meanings which can be attached to the equals sign. It is not suggested that primary-school children should be so made aware. Primary-school teachers may find it helpful to obtain a set of Dienes' Logical Blocks and to sort the blocks using such relations as:

has the same colour,
has the same thickness,
has the same shape, etc.

In this way the teacher becomes aware of the mathematics behind the simple processes of sorting in the infant classes and is better able to help in the discovery of relationships and in the building up of good mathematical language.

Equivalent Sets. Cardinal Number of a Set

It is now worth while considering in some detail what is involved in the idea of the cardinal number of a set. Consider the two sets A and B as shown.

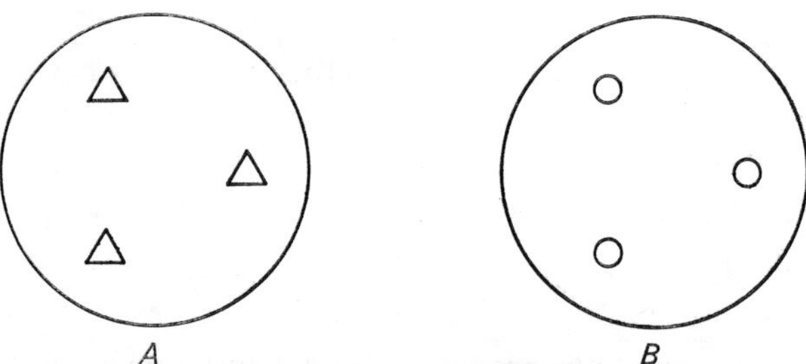

The elements of A can be matched one-to-one with the elements of B so that no element of A is matched to more than one element of B and vice versa. Also there are no elements of either set unmatched. Matching lines have been drawn to illustrate this.

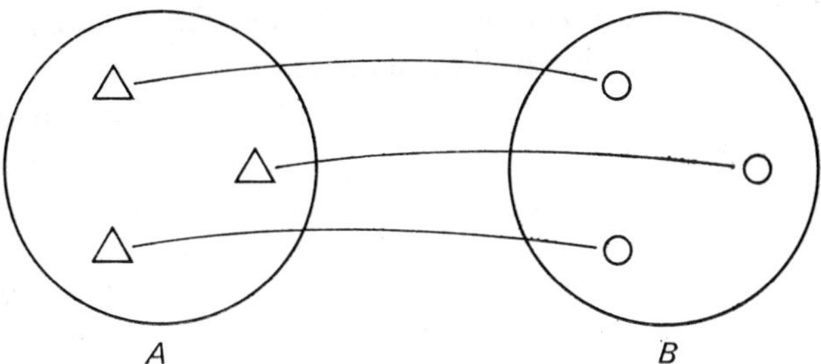

A and *B* are said to be *equivalent* sets. Thus equivalent sets are sets which contain the same number of elements. It is important to realize that the matching lines do not show the number. They only show that the sets have the same number. Cardinal number is an abstract property of a set.

Consider now the set *C* matched as shown with the set *B*.

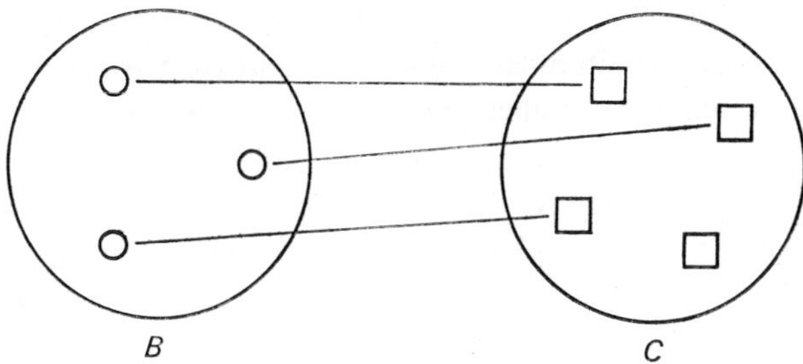

After matching has been carried out as far as possible there is still just one element of *C* unmatched. Thus *C* contains one more element than *B*. The idea of matching and having just one element left unmatched is the basis of the ordering of sets by their cardinality. This is also the basis of counting on in ones. Names must be chosen for the cardinal numbers of these ordered sets and symbols or *numerals* chosen to represent these names. Thus an English child must learn that the order of the names is one, two, three, four and not four, two, one, three, etc., whilst a German child would have to learn *eins*, *zwei*, *drei*, *vier*, etc. He must also learn that the numerals corresponding to these names are 1, 2, 3, 4, etc.

It is important for the student to realize that ability on the part of the child to repeat one, two, three, etc., does not mean that the process of counting is understood. Further, it is quite easy to show to a child a set of four elements but this is not showing him the number 4. We can record the fact using the numeral, 4, but we are still not showing the child the abstract number four. Only after a lot of experience of dealing with equivalent sets each containing four elements does he abstract the fourness of the sets. When counting a set of four objects some teachers hold up the first object and say "one". They then hold up the second and say "two", the third and say "three" and finally the fourth and say "four". This is not helping the child to understand. The teacher is in fact confusing the cardinal and the ordinal aspects of number. It is far better to hold up one object and say "one" and then to hold two objects together before saying "two", three objects together before saying "three" and so on.

The words first, second, third, fourth, etc., are ordinal numbers. When I stand on the third step of a flight of stairs I am only standing on one step but there are two steps below me. To find the cardinal number of a set the child matches the elements of the set with the names one, two, three, four, etc., and when he has matched all the elements in this way the cardinal number of the set is the last name that he has recited. Strictly it would have been better to have said "first, second, third, fourth, etc." This is rarely done in practice but it might help children to understand the concept of cardinal number if it were done.

The Infant Classroom Situation

It is probably true to say that in many infant schools there has been too great an emphasis on number relations in the past to the exclusion of other relationships and that children have been trying to do problems involving the operations of addition and subtraction before they had a very firm grasp of the abstract ideas involved in number. It is therefore suggested that the aim should be "to make haste slowly". In other words, a lot of time should be spent in the following ways:

(i) in developing a rich mathematical language (e.g. more than, less than, greater, smaller, larger, thinner, taller, wider, thicker, etc.);
(ii) looking for and discussing all kinds of relationships including number relationships but including also such things as "is the same shape", "is the same colour", "is taller than" and so on;
(iii) matching visibly with string and wool and drawing matching lines;
(iv) in practical activities, e.g. free and more directed play with water, sand, paints, ribbons, conkers, shells, buttons;
(v) weighing, measuring and shopping;
(vi) in recording discoveries made in connection with (iv) and (v);
(vii) fostering discussion through pictorial representation.

The role of the teacher is a vital one. Every opportunity must be taken for discussion and in providing rich and varied concrete experiences from which abstraction and discovery can take place. Though some parts of the day are often more specifically devoted to mathematics it is important to remember that at all times situations arise for developing mathematical ideas and vocabulary. The good teacher is aware that in Creative Activities, Music, Art, English, P.E., etc., there are many opportunities for mathematics to develop unobtrusively.

In the remainder of the chapter suggestions are given for some of the more directed activities which are designed to give greater understanding of number and other relationships. For ease of presentation the instructions are given in written form. The student should remember that the instructions will often be given verbally particularly if children are not able to read at that stage and that discussion and working with concrete objects must in all cases precede any written recording.

1. Sorting

A box or boxes of all kinds of objects suitable for sorting is an important piece of equipment in the infant classroom. The box might contain buttons, coloured beads, conkers, shells, toys, round, square and triangular shapes in various colours and sizes, hard objects and soft objects, etc. A box of Dienes' Logical Blocks is also an excellent piece of equipment for sorting. A handful of assorted objects is handed to the child with the simple instruction, "Sort those for me, please". The child should decide for himself in the first instance how to sort. Sometimes it will be by colour, sometimes by shape, sometimes by hard or soft, thick or thin, large or small and so on. Suggestions from the teacher at an appropriate moment enable situations to arise where there are almost endless possibilities for discovery and for the development of mathematical vocabulary and ideas. Questions can be asked such as "Why have you sorted like that? Are there more in that set than this? Are there fewer red beads than yellow ones?" It must be noted that this is a pre-counting stage and it must be quite obvious to the child *without counting* whether there are fewer in one set than the other.

The child could record when appropriate by drawing a simple kind of Venn diagram, thus:

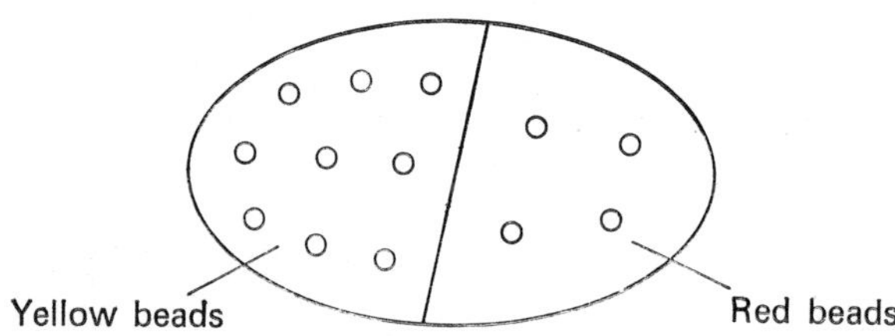

2. Comparing two or more objects for size

(i) Put a mark *over* the larger ball. Put a mark *on* the smaller ball. Put a mark *under* the smaller ball.

The above are suggestions for instructions.

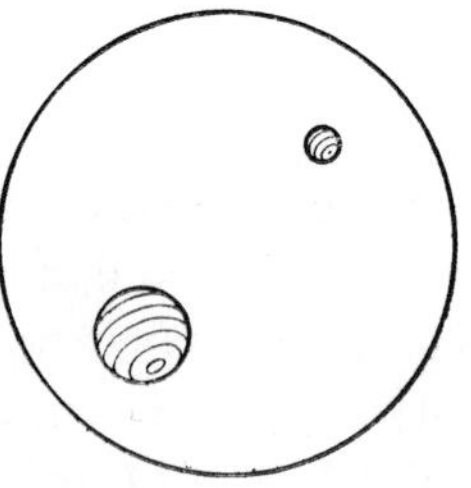

(ii) Mark the largest shape.

Mark the smallest toy.

3. Comparing in the same way for height

Mark the tallest tree.

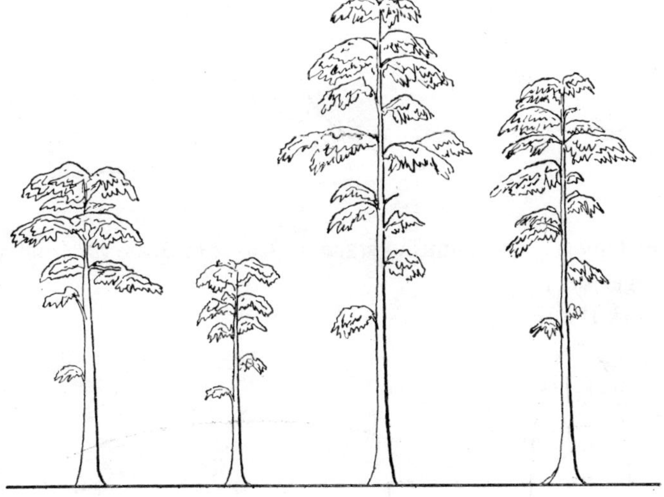

4. The same development can be used for measurement

Mark the longest piece of string.
Mark the shortest piece of string.

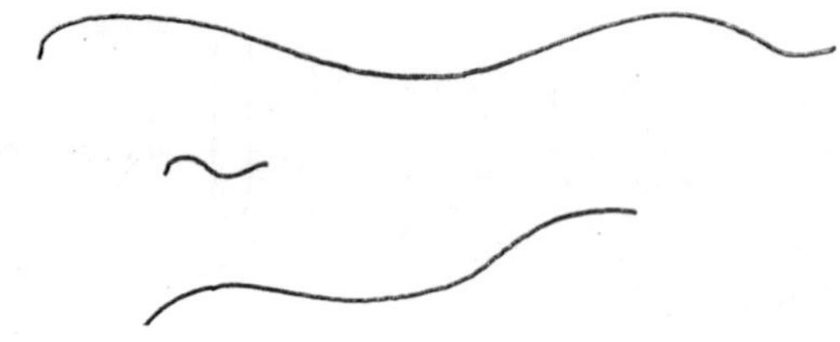

5. Comparing sets

(i) Mark the larger set.

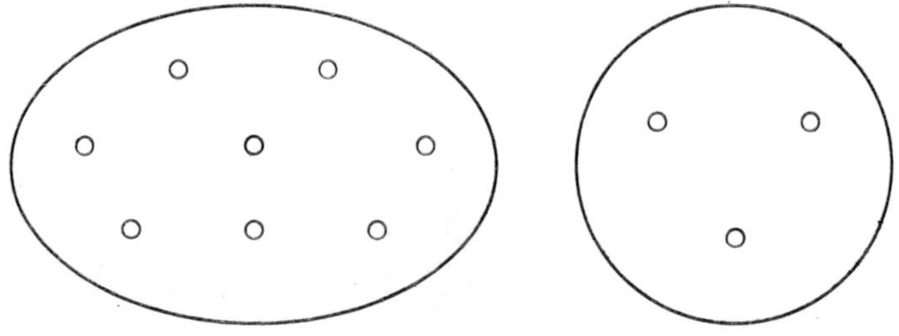

(*Note*. This is a pre-counting stage and so it must be obvious which is the larger set.)

(ii) Mark the smaller set.

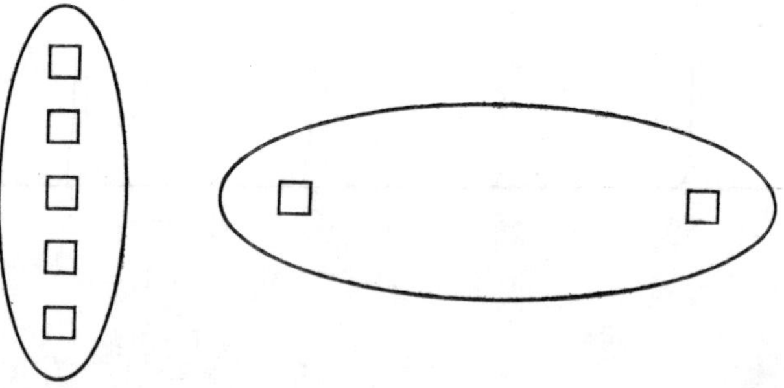

6. (i) Without counting draw a set in the space which has more objects.

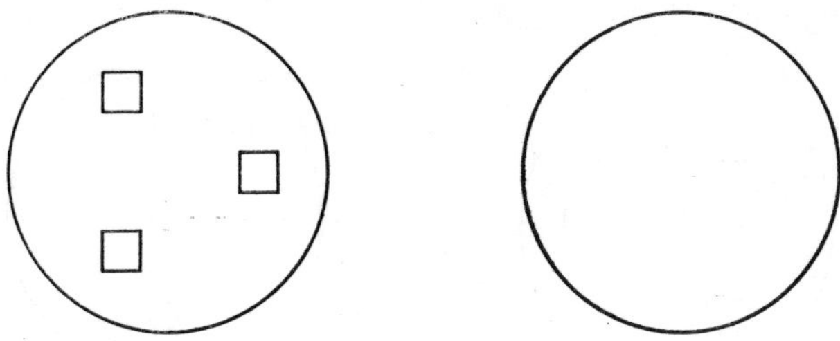

(ii) The same development for less.

(*Note* that as with all these suggestions the activities are done first with concrete objects placed on plates or in boxes or in closed loops of string.)

7. Draw matching lines (or join with pieces of wool when using real objects).

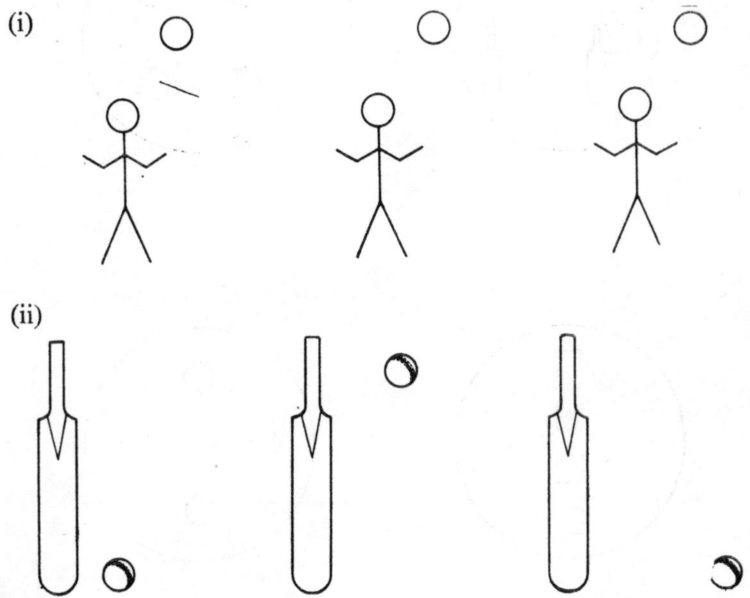

Note. No number names at this stage.

8.

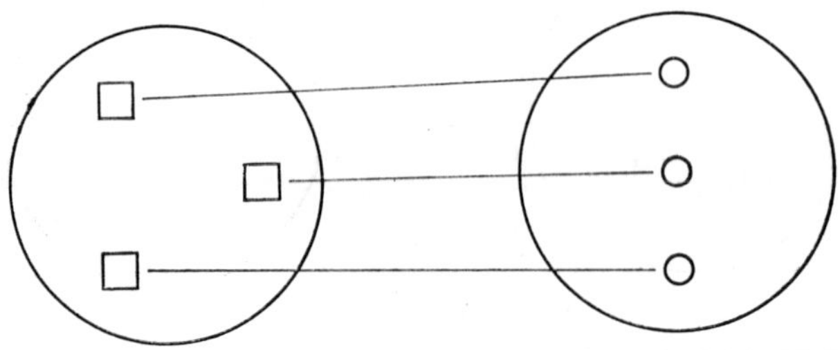

The lines show that both sets have the same number.
(*Note for the student*. They do not show the number.) You draw lines.

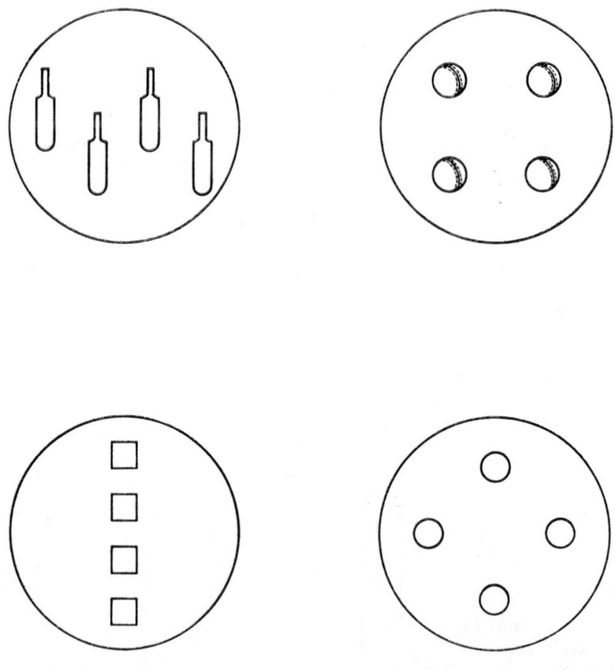

9. (i) Give each bat a ball.

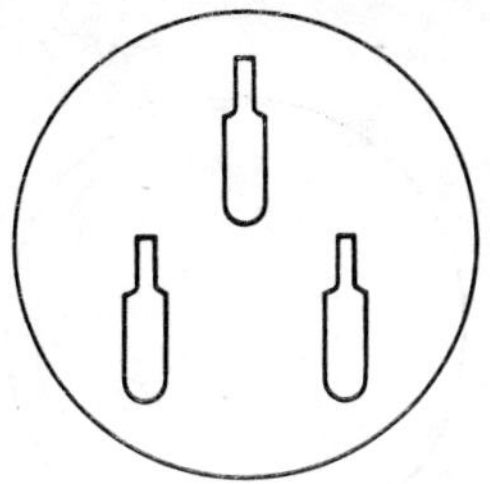
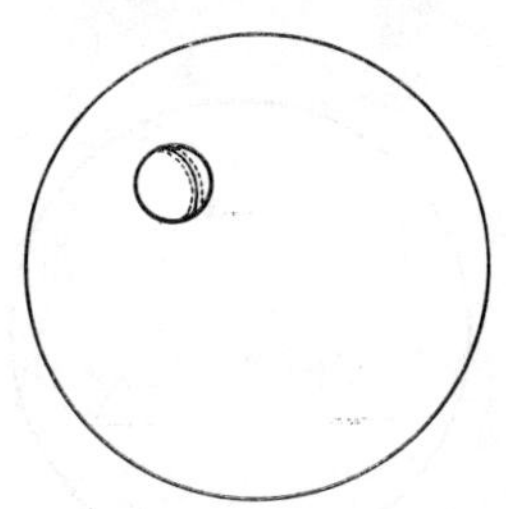

(ii) Give each man a hat.

10. Match the sets one-to-one to see if the sets have the same number.

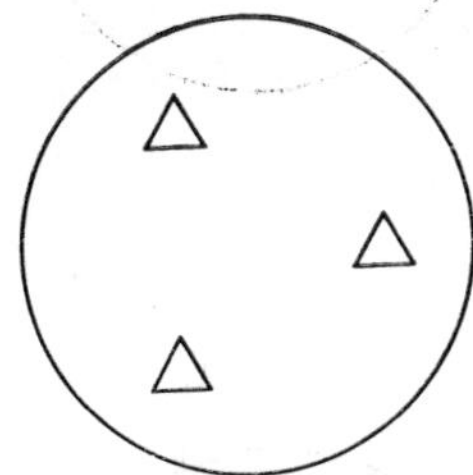
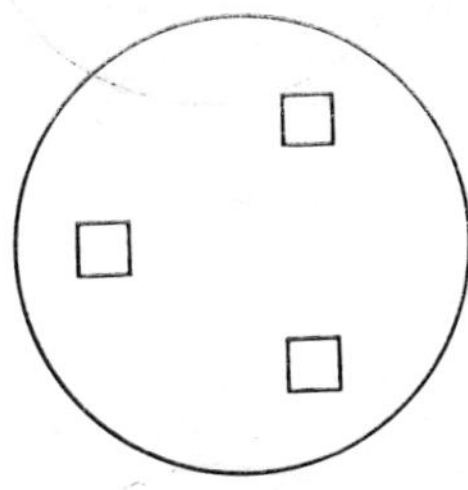

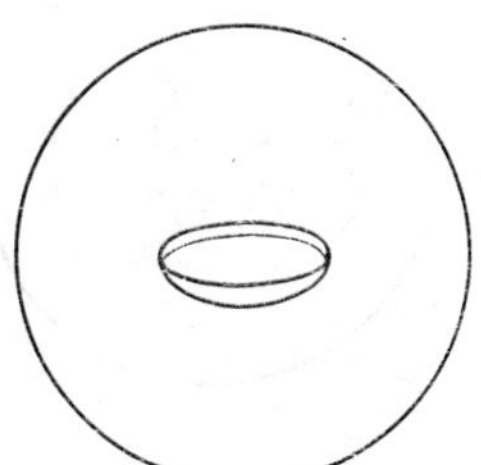

11. Draw a set which has the same number.

(i)

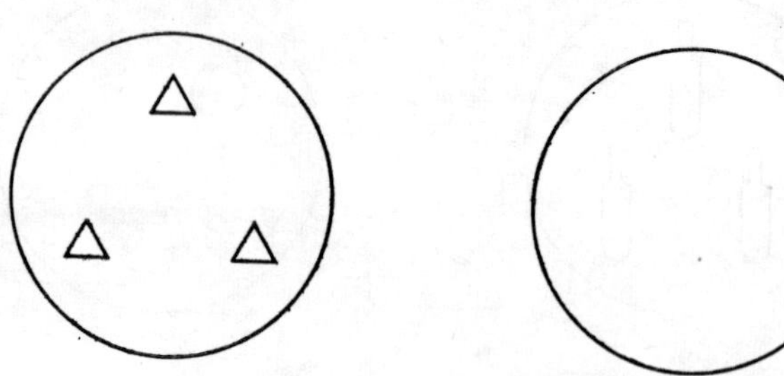

(ii)

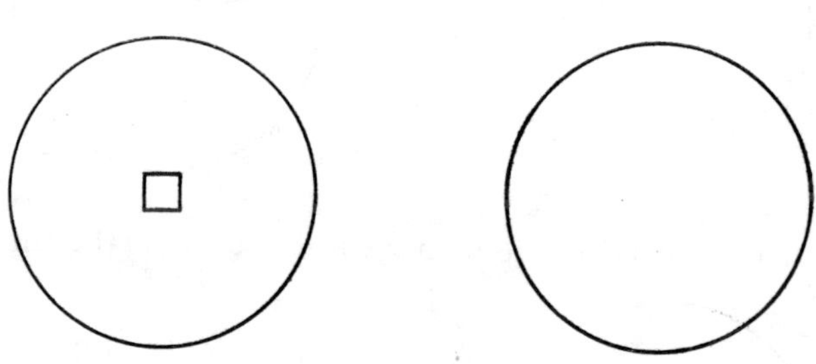

(iii)

12. Draw a line from bat to ball. Which set has the more? Draw a ball for the extra bat.

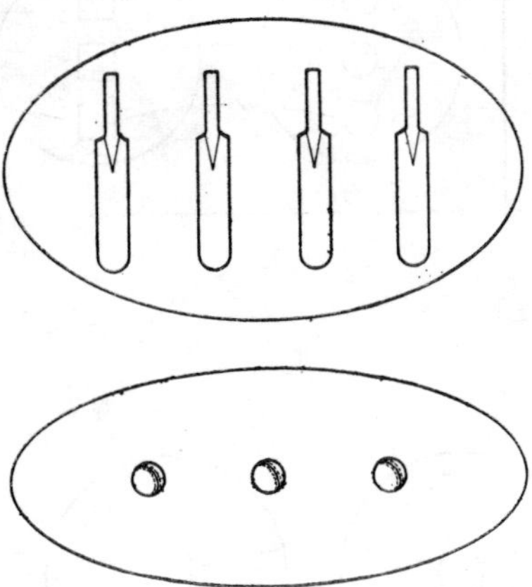

13. Draw sets which have one more element than the given set.

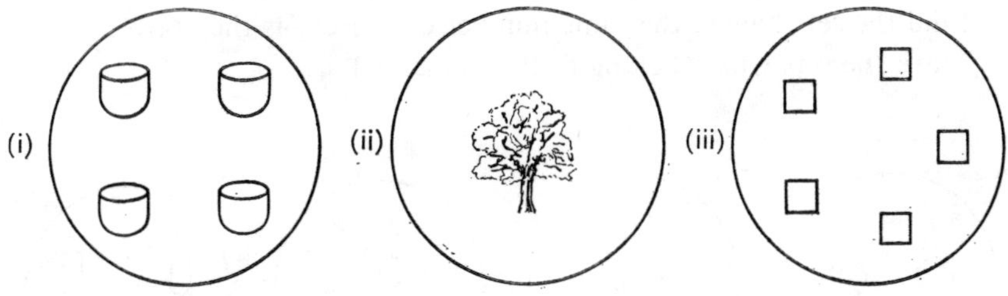

14. Introduction to the numeral needed to record the cardinal number of the set.

The numerals 1, 2, 3 and 4 should be drawn on separate cards and the child is instructed to place the appropriate numeral by the set.

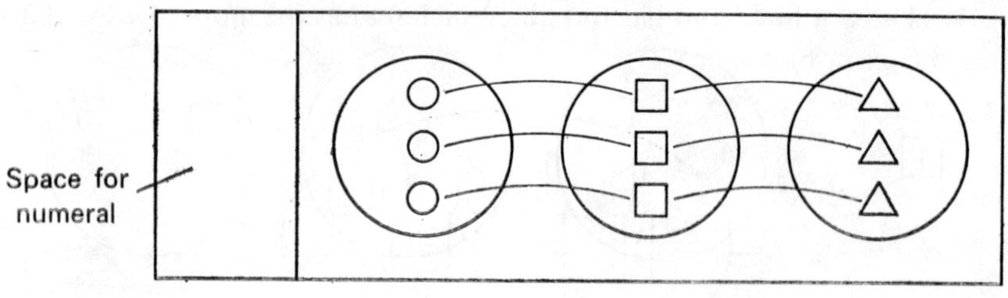

15.

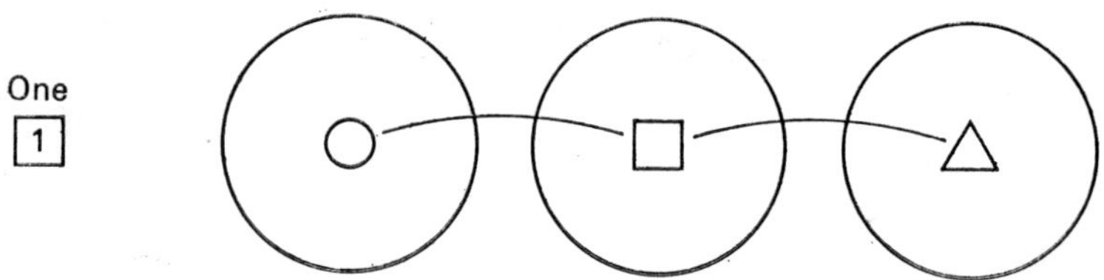

All the sets have one object.
Find the sets having the same number of objects as the above.
Mark the sets which belong to the numeral 1.

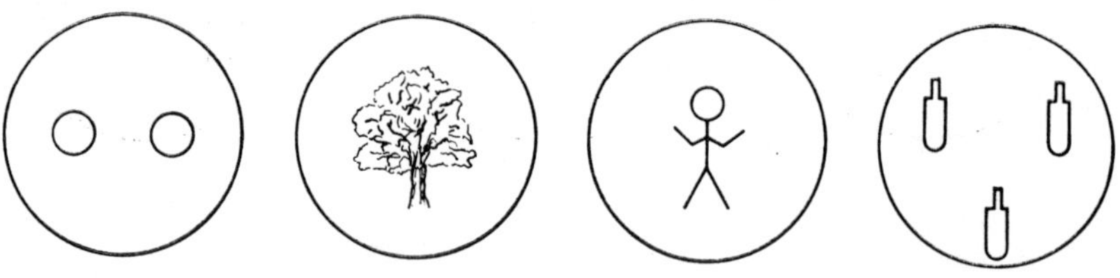

Repeat the above for numerals 2, 3 and 4. Most children are able to recognize sets of one, two, three or four objects without counting.

16.

3

Point out to the child that 1 instructs him to find the set containing one object and so on. Mark the sets in the row which correspond with the numeral on the left of the row.

Next mark all sets which correspond to the numeral 1, then to the numerals 2, 3 and 4.

17.

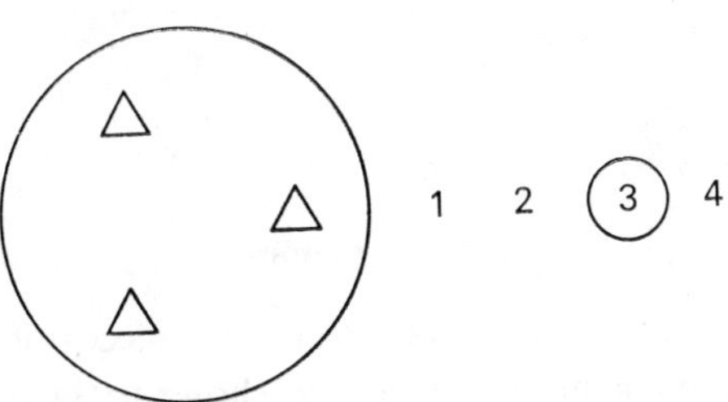

Ring the numeral for the set.

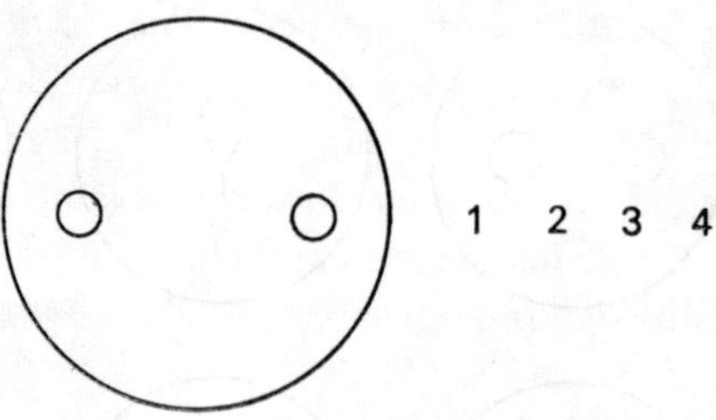

18. Continue the development for sets containing one more object than the given set and numeral recognition for the numerals 5, 6, 7 and so on.

It might be helpful to mention two other activities that are well worth while, namely the playing of number games and the setting out of trays of objects.

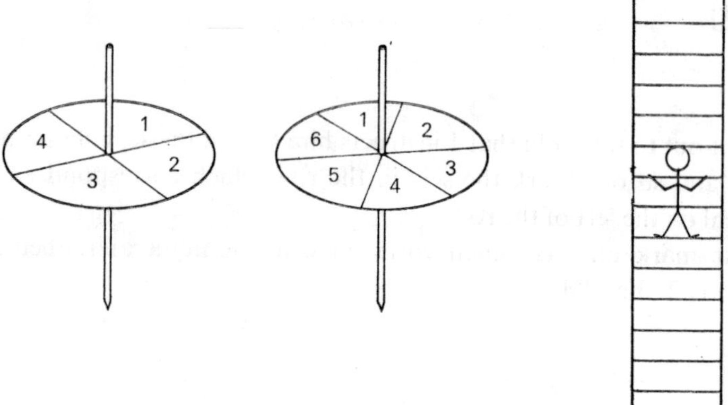

Number Games

Simple spinners can be made out of circular pieces of cardboard and wooden meat skewers or similar objects, as shown in the diagram. Models can be made out of pipe cleaners and simple cardboard ladders.

Two children play the game by spinning the card until it comes to rest with a numeral in contact with the desk. The "pipe-cleaner man" is placed on the appropriate rung of the ladder. The children are encouraged to discuss the situations with such language as: "My man is higher than yours," or, "Your man is two rungs lower than mine." Not every throw need be recorded. Home-made dice can be used instead of the spinners when the numerals to six are known.

Trays of Objects

It is also useful to have in the infant room cardboard or metal trays in the corners of which are the numerals. The child will place on the tray the correct number of objects. One day six conkers will be placed in the tray with the numeral 6 in the corner. Another day it will be six dinky toys, another six shells and another six sweets. It is important that the children are able to handle concrete objects and that those who have not yet got a certain skill can benefit by watching other children putting out the trays for the day.

Partitioning Sets

When a child understands the concept of number a lot of time can be spent allowing him to partition sets of real objects and recording his findings. For example, if a set of five dinky cars is partitioned into two sets he could discover that the sets might contain respectively one and four objects or two and three or three and two or four and one. At this stage it is probably more useful to record these facts thus:

$$1,4 \xrightarrow{\text{altogether}} 5$$

$$2,3 \xrightarrow{\text{altogether}} 5$$

$$3,2 \xrightarrow{\text{altogether}} 5$$

$$4,1 \xrightarrow{\text{altogether}} 5$$

Later the recording might be $1,4 \xrightarrow{\text{add}} 5$

and then $1,4 \xrightarrow{+} 5$

and finally $1+4 = 5$.

Before a more detailed study of counting number bonds and their extension is undertaken the student will find it helpful to consider in some detail the Hindu–Arabic system of recording of numbers. This is done in the next chapter and further consideration of number bonds is dealt with in Chapter 5.

CHAPTER 4

RECORDING OF NUMBER AND USE OF DIFFERENT BASES

RECALL that cardinal number is an abstract property of a set. The sets which are illustrated below can be put into one-to-one correspondence with each other, i.e. each member of the first set can be matched one-to-one with each member of the second set. There are no members unmatched. Thus the sets have the same cardinal number. Note that the matching lines only show that the sets have the same cardinal number. They do not show the number. Number is an abstract property.

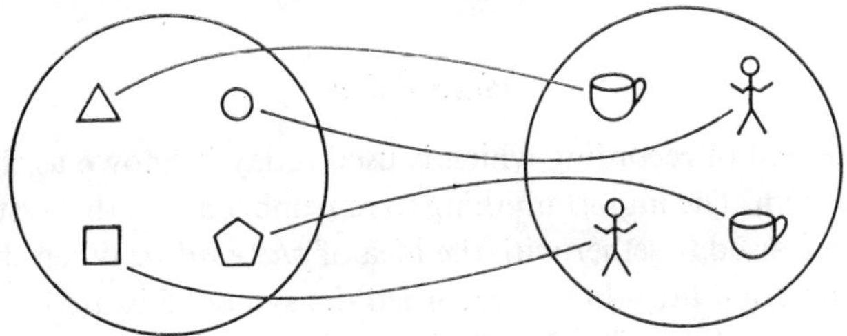

The sets can also be matched with a standard series as shown. We see from this that the cardinal number in this case is four.

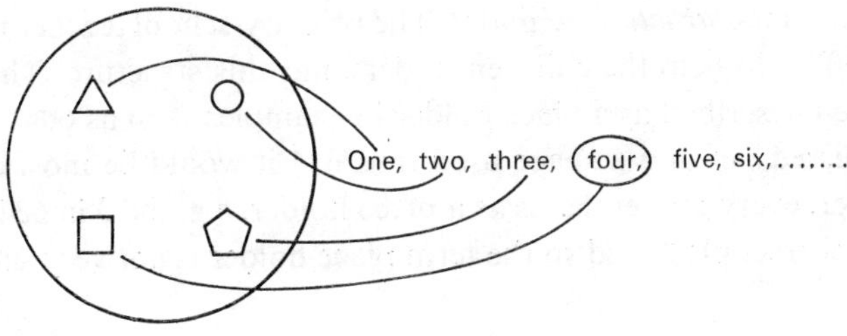

There are various ways of recording the cardinal number. The Romans might have recorded it using the numeral IV. They would have recorded the *number* five by the *numeral* V.

Q. 1. How would the Romans have recorded the numbers (i) eighty-two, (ii) two hundred and fifty-four?

2. What numbers do the following symbols stand for: (i) MCCCLXXII, (ii) DCCXIX?

A. 1. (i) LXXXII, (ii) CCLIV.

2. (i) One thousand three hundred and seventy-two, (ii) seven hundred and nineteen.

Note that the Roman system of recording does not use place value. Thus in question 1 (i) the three "X's" all have the value of ten even though they follow one another. In question 1 (ii), however, the I before the V does mean one less than five so that the position of the numerals does make a difference even in this system. The student should try to find other systems of recording which do not use "place value".

Place Value

The method of recording which is used today is known as the Hindu-Arabic system. The important thing to remember about this system is that a *base ten* is used together with the idea of *place value*. When the number five hundred and fifty-three is recorded the symbol 5 is used for both the five hundred and the fifty. The position of the 5 relative to the other symbols determines its value. Adults are so familiar with this system that they are inclined to forget that it takes some children a long time to understand the *structure* behind it. The primary-school teacher must make every effort to help the children understand this structure. The numeral 0 is often described as a place holder in examples such as 604. If the zero were missed out and a space used thus 6 4 it would be most confusing. However, every numeral acts as a place holder, e.g. the 3 in 634 holds the 6 in its correct place and so the term place holder is not very satisfactory.

Bases Other Than Ten

Because it is essential that children really understand place value and base ten it is helpful that they should work with bases other than ten in the primary school. When recording in base ten only ten symbols are needed, viz. 0, 1, 2, 3, 4, 5, 6, 7, 8, 9. When using base four, for example, only four symbols are needed, viz. 0, 1, 2, 3, whilst when using base two (known as Binary) only two symbols 0 and 1 are needed. It is sometimes argued that children in the secondary school should use binary because computers use binary. This is not the reason for using other bases in the primary school. They are used to focus attention on the understanding and structure of the base ten system. For this reason it is not recommended that Junior school children should be introduced to binary as the first alternate base to ten. In many ways binary has its own difficulties because it has only two symbols. Base four, six or even three should be used before binary with middle Juniors. Top Juniors can get a lot of pleasure, and in mathematics we must have pleasure, from investigating the use of binary in conjunction with punched cards and sorting.

Base Six

We probably use base ten because we were born with four fingers and a thumb on each hand whereas if we had been born with only two fingers and a thumb we might have used base six. We might also have used different names for the cardinal numbers of sets. The name forty-five suggests four tens and five units though the name eleven does not suggest one ten and one unit. Students often are confused between the name and the abstract property. When students meet base six for the first time there is often the reaction, "You can't have fifteen in base six!" It is true that the cardinal number of a set containing fifteen objects would probably not be given the name fifteen had base six been in common use, but it is obviously possible to have a set containing so many objects.

Q. Record the following numbers using base six: (i) six, (ii) seven, (iii) twelve, (iv) thirty-three, (v) thirty-six.

A. (i) 10, (ii) 11, (iii) 20, (iv) 53, (v) 100.

It should be remembered that children encounter even greater difficulties as they try to master base ten than the reader did in trying to answer these questions. It is possible that some readers were tempted to write 56 as the solution to part (v) above. Remember that in base six only six symbols, namely 0, 1, 2, 3, 4, 5, are used in the recording just as in base ten the symbols used are 0, 1, 2, 3, 4, 5, 6, 7, 8, 9.

Q. (i) What number is represented by 3245 in base six?
(ii) What is the base six representation of four hundred and fifty-seven?
(iii) What number is represented by 3234 in base four?
(iv) Make up some similar questions for a friend and check your results together.

A. (i) $(3\times 6^3)+(2\times 6^2)+(4\times 6)+5$,
i.e. six hundred and forty-eight + seventy-two + twenty-four + five,
i.e. seven hundred and forty-nine.
(ii) 2041.
(iii) 3234 is impossible when using base four. Remember the symbol 4 cannot be used in base four.

When using base ten children often head the columns by h, t, u to show hundreds, tens, and units. A more sophisticated way of doing this would have been to write 10^2, 10, 1 or even 10^2, 10^1, 10^0.*

Reading from right to left instead of left to right it would be 10^0, 10^1, 10^2, 10^3, . . .

In base six the columns would be 6^0, 6^1, 6^2, 6^3, . . . (This is not strictly correct for the symbol 6 ought not to have been used in base six. In fact the headings are still recorded as 10^0, 10^1, 10^2, . . . where this is taken to be read as one, six, thirty-six, etc.)

* Remember that $10^3 = 10\times 10\times 10$ or 3 tens multiplied together.
$10^2 = 10\times 10$ or two tens multiplied together.
Hence $10^3\times 10^2$ is 5 tens multiplied together or 10^5. More generally $10^a\times 10^b = 10^{a+b}$ when a and b are natural numbers. Clearly 10^0 does not mean no tens multiplied together. What meaning, if any, can be given to 10^0? Assuming that the law $10^a\times 10^b = 10^{a+b}$ still holds when $b = 0$ we see that $10^a\times 10^0 = 10^{a+0} = 10^a$. But $10^a\times 1 = 10^a$ and so the meaning for 10^0 is clearly 1, i.e. $10^0 = 1$.

In a similar way it can be shown that $6^0 = 1$ or $x^0 = 1$ for any x.

Number Bases for Junior Children

It is advisable to introduce children to bases other than ten in the middle Juniors. Remember that the aim is to help them to understand the structure of the Hindu–Arabic system involving place value and the inter-relationships between the values of the different columns. It is important to remember also that children abstract from the concrete and learn by doing. Structural apparatus, be it home-made or commercially produced, should be available for the children to use as long as they feel the need for it. (Do not force them to use the apparatus once they are keen to discard it.) Apparatus which could be used is as follows:

1. Dienes' Multibase Arithmetic Blocks are strongly recommended. Information on the use of these blocks is given in several books published by Z. P. Dienes.

2. A simple abacus may be used. It can be constructed as shown in the figure by fixing dowel rods into a piece of wood.

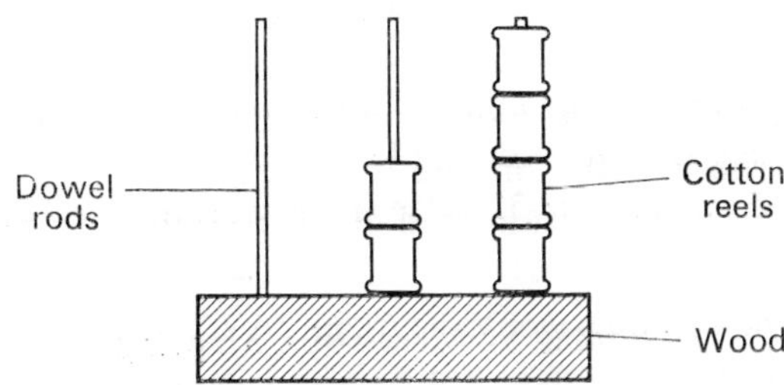

Empty cotton reels slide on to the rods. A different abacus is needed for each base for it is advisable to make the lengths of the rods just long enough to take four cottons reels in base five, five cotton reels for base six and so on.

3. At a later stage coloured cubes may be used with different exchange values for different colours. Thus, for example, using base three we might suggest that three red cubes can be exchanged for one yellow, three yellows for one green and so on.

4. Instead of the cubes squared paper may be used cut into squares, strips, larger squares and so on.

Children's Activities

1. Give a handful of spills (or straws) to the children. Instruct them to fasten into bundles of four with rubber bands. Record the number of bundles and the number of spills left over. (Do not give more than fifteen spills in the handful.) Show the recording on the abacus for base four.

2. Put out the number of spills corresponding to the number shown on the abacus below:

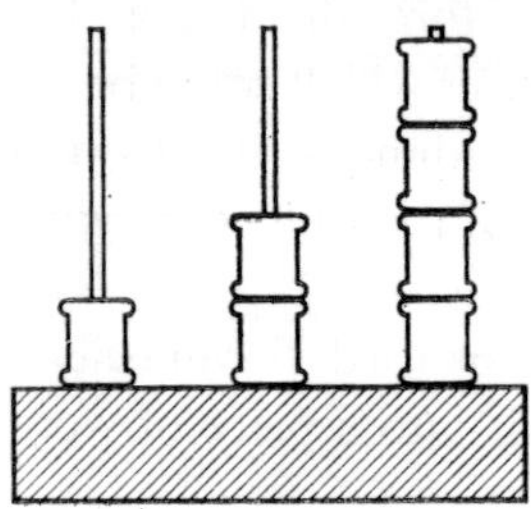

3. Show on the abacus the number which in base six is recorded as 35.

4. Repeat as above using different bases.

5. How would the number 35 (base six) be recorded in base ten?

Recording by Means of a Mapping

When children have a good understanding of the recording of numbers in different bases it is useful to record by means of a mapping as shown in the figure.

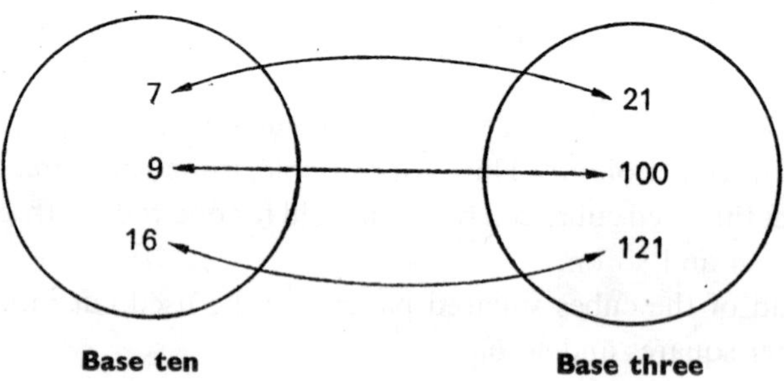

Test your understanding of different bases by answering the following questions:

Q. 1. Complete the diagram shown below.

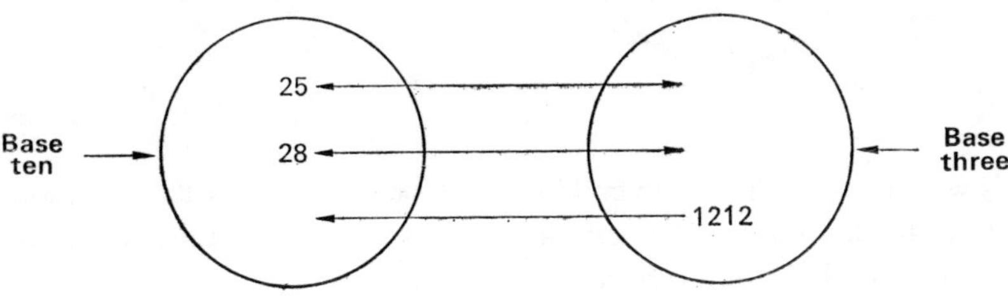

2. Complete the following diagram.

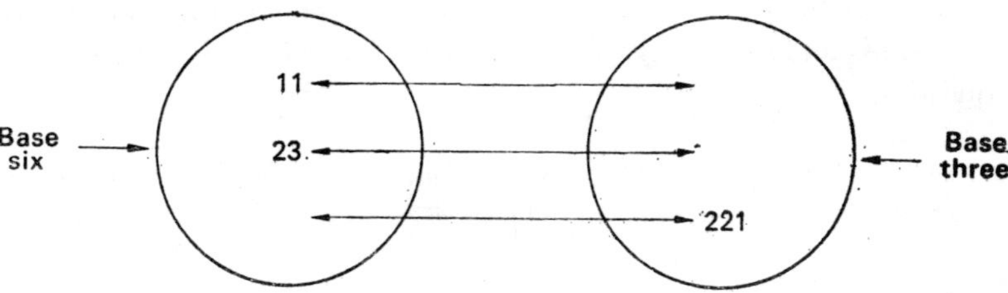

A. 1.

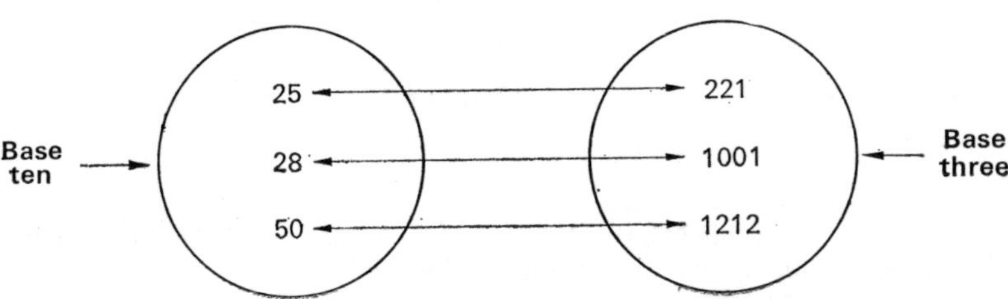

2.

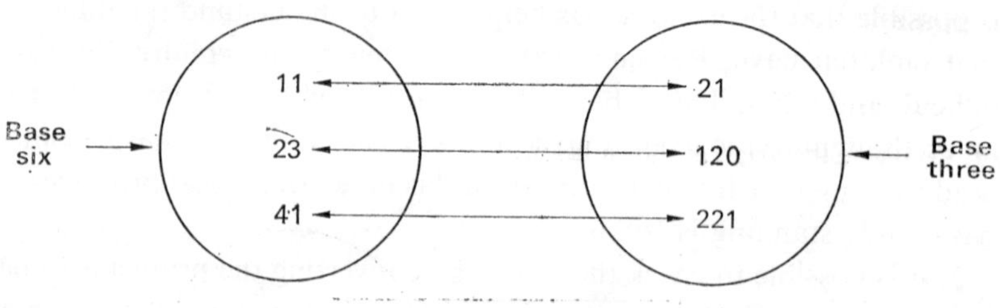

It is worth noting that when children are able to record as above without using structural material to help them the teacher has an interesting way of testing multiplication facts at his disposal.

Operations Using Bases Other Than Ten

Although the operations of addition, multiplication, subtraction and division are dealt with in greater detail in later chapters the reader may like to test his understanding of work in other bases by doing the following questions.

Q. 1. The operation in each of the following is addition. Complete the calculations.

(i) Base six	341 133 —— ——	(ii) Base six	341 245 —— ——
(iii) Base four	323 . . . —— 1231	(iv) Base five	444 . . . —— 1222

2. The operation in each of the following is subtraction. Complete the calculations.

(i) Base five.	341 133 —— ——	(ii) Base six	341 245 —— ——
(iii) Base five	341 . . . —— 122	(iv) Base six	444 . . . —— 151

A. 1. (i) 514, (ii) 1030, (iii) 302, (iv) 223. **2.** (i) 203, (ii) 52, (iii) 214, (iv) 253.
As a result of doing these calculations, various points arise.

---

1. Did you find any of the above questions difficult? If you did, then it is possible that the exercise has helped you to understand the difficulties that children have. Remember that base ten to the children is just as difficult and unfamiliar as base six is to adults who have not really given much thought to the recording of number. The adult mind has become so used to using base ten that calculations become mechanical processes and basic understanding is lacking.

2. It is possible to check the results by converting the problems to base ten in each case. (*Note*. We are really mapping each number on to its image in base ten.) It is further possible that some readers did the problems this way, i.e. they mapped each number on to its base ten image, did the problem in base ten and finally mapped the solution in base ten back on to its appropriate base image. This method should be discouraged. It does not help in the understanding of the structure behind the number system which is a vital aim. Remember that ability to perform mechanical tricks without understanding is not to be encouraged. Increase the POWER SKILLS of children and the SPEED SKILLS will follow.

3. In question 2 (iii) did you use the fact that the open sentence

$$341-\square = 122 \Leftrightarrow 341 = \square+122 \Leftrightarrow 341-122 = \square\ ?$$

Note. The sign $\Leftrightarrow$ means "if and only if" (sometimes written as iff). It is a powerful sign in the sense that it means that an argument is reversible. It would be wrong to use this sign in the following example: $x = 16 \Leftrightarrow x^2 = 256$. It is certainly true that if $x = 16$ then $x^2 = 256$ but it is not true that if $x^2 = 256$ then $x = 16$ for x might be -16. The correct sign to use in this case is $\Rightarrow$. Thus it is correct to write $x = 16 \Rightarrow x^2 = 256$ which means that if $x = 16$ then $x^2 = 256$ or $x = 16$ implies that $x^2 = 256$.

Q. Which sign, $\Rightarrow$ or $\Leftrightarrow$, would be correct in the following statements?

1. The sides of a rectangle are 2 cm and 8 cm ▭, the area of the rectangle is 16 square centimetres.

2. The side of a square is 4 cm □, the area of the square is 16 square centimetres.

A. 1. $\Rightarrow$. It would be quite wrong to use $\Leftrightarrow$ since the sides of the rectangle need not be 2 cm and 8 cm if the area were 16 sq. cm.

2. Either sign could be used but it would be better to use $\Leftrightarrow$ which reminds us that not only is it true that if the side of a square is 4 cm then the area is 16 square centimetres but it is also true that if the square is 16 square centimetres then the side is 4 cm.

The importance of the fact that children should know that $3-1 = 2 \Leftrightarrow 3 = 2+1$ is dealt with later in the book.

4. In finding the solutions to the subtraction questions there are basically two different approaches to the problem known as "the decomposition approach" and "the equal addition approach". There are, of course, many other ways of obtaining solutions and children should be encouraged to be flexible in their approach and to discover for themselves methods of solution. However, there will be a stage when the teacher will wish to consolidate and teach *with understanding* either the decomposition or equal addition methods or both. It is very important for the reader to realize the value of purity of language. Unfortunately many teachers resort to phrases like "borrow and pay back" which do not help children to understand the basic ideas. Many teachers assert that it is easier to teach "decomposition" than "equal addition" with understanding. It is easy for both methods to be understood if sufficient care is taken in the explanations.

Consider the open sentence*

$$53-28 = \square$$

This is an abstract problem. It might have arisen from any of the following:

(i) There are 53 conkers in a bag; 28 are removed. How many are left in the bag? (This is really taking away 28 from 53.)

(ii) There are 53 people in one room and 28 in another. How many more are there in the first room than in the second? (This is *not* taking away. It is impossible to "take away" the 28 from the 53. The problem here is one of finding the difference betwen 53 and 28.)

(iii) There are 28 people already sitting on chairs in the room. How many more people may sit down if there are 53 chairs altogether

* See Chapter 5.

in the room? (This is really "complementary addition". This kind of situation often arises in the giving of change in shops.)

When the solution to the open sentence is known then clearly the solutions to the three problems are known but it does not follow that a child will realize that the solutions are known. It is vital that children should be given experiences showing that the minus sign is used for different thought processes. When a child has not this understanding of the various aspects of the use of the minus sign it is not only pointless for a teacher to say, "You can do it John, it's only a *take away sum*", when in fact finding the difference is involved; it is also very misleading. It is impossible to stress too greatly the need for purity of language on the part of the teacher.

It is probable that the method known as decomposition can be more easily understood from a "take away" situation and that the equal addition method from a "finding the difference" situation.

Decomposition

Consider the problem of 53 conkers in the bag. When written as the open sentence $53-28 = \square$ or in the form

$$\begin{array}{r} 53 \\ -28 \\ \hline \\ \hline \end{array}$$

we have 5 sets of ten and three units from which we wish to remove 2 sets of ten and eight units. Since it is impossible to remove eight units from three we must first decompose one of the 5 tens into ten units, i.e. we write 53 not as $50+3$ but as $40+13$. It is then quite staightforward to remove 8 of the 13 leaving 5 units and removing 2 sets of ten from the 4 sets of ten leaving 2 sets of ten.

The method is illustrated by:

$$\begin{aligned} 53-28 &= (50+3)-(20+8) \\ &= (40+13)-(20+8) \\ &= 20+5 = 25. \end{aligned}$$

Equal Addition

Consider now the problem of 53 people in one room and 28 in another and the difference in numbers is required. If there were 10 more people in each room the difference would remain the same. This is the principle involved in the method of "equal addition". Although the number ten was chosen to be added to the two numbers whose difference was required the principle would have been the same had any number been added instead of ten.

Using this principle we obtain:

$$\begin{aligned} 53-28 &= (50+3)-(20+8) \\ &= (50+13)-(30+8) \\ &= (50-30)+(13-8) \\ &= 20+5 \\ &= 25 \end{aligned}$$

It should be noted that the first number 53 has been increased by ten by adding ten units to the three units whilst the second number has been increased by ten in the form of a set of ten, i.e. the 2 tens have been increased to 3 tens.

It is true that the thought process involved in this method is more difficult to understand than in the previous "decomposition method". Before this method is introduced formally the children should have had a lot of experience in extending the number bonds.

Thus:

$$\begin{aligned} 8+7 &= 15 \Leftrightarrow 15-8 = 7 \\ 18+7 &= 25 \Leftrightarrow 25-18 = 7 \\ 28+7 &= 35 \Leftrightarrow 35-28 = 7, \text{ etc.} \end{aligned}$$

and thus:

$$\begin{aligned} 8+7 &= 15 \Leftrightarrow 15-8 = 7 \\ 9+7 &= 16 \Leftrightarrow 16-9 = 7 \\ 10+7 &= 17 \Leftrightarrow 17-10 = 7, \text{ etc.} \end{aligned}$$

The reader should also note that this is a good example of the use of pattern to draw attention to an important idea.

Reminder. 1. In all the work involving either base ten or any other base home-made or commercially manufactured material should be available *as long as the children need it*.

2. Abstract from concrete situations whenever possible.

3. Use other bases to help the children to understand the structure of the base ten system.

Multiplication in Different Bases

Since we use different bases to give understanding and not to set more complicated examples, there is little if any point in doing examples involving multiplication by a number greater than the base (except in the case of binary). Multiplication by the base is, however, worth while.

Q. Multiply any number in base three by three. Repeat with a different number What do you notice? Explain why this is so.

A. e.g. 121 in base three multiplied by three gives 1210.

If your explanation was: "I added a nought" then this is NOT a satisfactory explanation.

121 in base three means 1 unit and 2 threes and 1 nine.
1 unit multiplied by three is 1 three,
2 threes multiplied by three is 2 nines,
1 nine multiplied by three is 1 twenty-seven.

Thus each symbol now occupies one place to the left of its original position and the number is 1 twenty-seven plus 2 nines plus 1 three plus zero units, i.e. 1210.

Reminder. Avoid slipshod language and careless explanations which are misleading to children.

Algorithm for Changing to Base Ten from Base Four and vice versa

The following methods may be used for changing bases.

Remember that they should not be given to children as a "trick" for them to remember. They may be used as interesting puzzles for children to discover why they work. The reader should try to find out why they give correct results before reading the explanation.

(i) *Base Four to Base Ten*

What is the base ten representation of the number which in base four is recorded as 321?

Method:

$$\begin{array}{ccc} 3 & 2 & 1 \\ \times\ \underline{4} & \underline{12} & \underline{56} \\ 12 & 14 & 57 \\ & \times\ \underline{4} & \\ & 56 & \end{array}$$

i.e. $(321)_{\text{base four}} \leftrightarrow (57)_{\text{base ten}}$

(ii) *Base Ten to Base Four*

What is the base four representation of the number which in base ten is recorded as 43?

Method:

4 | 43
4 | 10 remainder 3
4 | 2 remainder 2
0 remainder 2

Hence $(43)_{\text{base ten}} \leftrightarrow (223)_{\text{base four}}$

Explanation: (i) $57 = 56+1$
$= 4\times(12+2)+1$
$= (4\times4\times3)+(4\times2)+1$
$= 4^2\times3+4\times2+1$

(ii) $43 = 4\times10+3$
$= 4\times(4\times2+2)+3$
$= 4^2\times2+4\times2+3$

Binary (Base Two)

Reminder. It is not advisable to introduce primary school children to binary before they have used many bases other than ten. The fact that there are only two symbols, viz. 0 and 1, in binary can be confusing. The aim in using bases other than ten and two is to focus attention on the structure of the number system.

It is worth studying binary for the following reasons:

(i) Primary-school children of age 10 or 11 obtain much pleasure from investigating binary.

(ii) It can be used in conjunction with punched cards in the classification of shapes using various properties.

(iii) Top Juniors and secondary-school children are interested in binary because of its use in computers.

(iv) Students in training and teachers themselves are able to understand children's difficulties as they are confronted for the first time with bicimals (binary decimals).

A class discussion on number patterns was taking place and the following recordings of children's examples had been made on the blackboard by the teacher.

2, 4, 6, 8, 10, . . .

1, 3, 5, 7, 9, . . .

1, 4, 9, 16, 25, . . .

1, 3, 6, 10, 15, . . .

1, 2, 4, 8, 16, . . .

At this stage the teacher asked the children to look at the last sequence and to see if by combining members of this set using addition only it were possible to express all numbers. This was doubted by some of the members of the class. One boy said, "Let's try it out. Give us one."

The teacher gave the number eleven and they discovered that eleven could be represented by $8+2+1$. This was immediately followed by the children giving numbers to the rest of the class for them to find a solution. The first few numbers given were 13, 9, 15 and it was discovered that all could be represented.

$$13 = 8+4+1,$$
$$9 = 8+1,$$
$$15 = 8+4+2+1.$$

This gave an immediate lead into binary notation.

$11 = 8+2+1 = (1\times8)+(0\times4)+(1\times2)+(1\times1)$ and in binary eleven is recorded as 1011.

In the same way we have:

Thirteen is $(1\times8)+(1\times4)+(0\times2)+(1\times1)$ and in binary representation thirteen is 1101.

Fifteen is $(1\times8)+(1\times4)+(1\times2)+(1\times1)$ and in binary representation fifteen is 1111.

Q. 1. Record the numbers one to ten in the binary notation.
2. What is the binary representation of (i) thirty-one, (ii) thirty-three?
3. What is the number whose binary representation is 110101?

A. 1. 1, 10, 11, 100, 101, 110, 111, 1000, 1001, 1010.
2. (i) 11111 (sixteen + eight + four + two + one), (ii) 100001.
3. Fifty-three. [$(1\times32)+(1\times16)+(0\times8)+(1\times4)+(0\times2)+1$, i.e. $32+16+4+1 = = 53$.]

An advantage of binary is that very few number facts need to be known. They are:

$$1+0 = 0+1 = 1,$$
$$1+1 = 10,$$
$$1\times0 = 0\times1 = 0,$$
$$0\times0 = 0.$$

Q. Record five and thirteen in binary. Find the sum and product of five and thirteen using binary notation.
Repeat with any two other numbers and check your results in base ten.

A.

```
five          101  (i.e. 1 four+1 unit)
thirteen     1101  (i.e. 1 eight+1 four+1 unit)

              101
          +  1101
          -------
            10010  (i.e. 1 sixteen+1 two = eighteen)

              101
          ×  1101
          -------
              101  (i.e. 1 four+1 unit = 1 five)
             0000  (i.e. zero          = 0 fives)
            10100  (i.e. 1 sixteen+1 four = four fives)
           101000  (i.e. 1 thirty-two+1 eight = eight fives)
          -------
          1000001  (i.e. 1 sixty-four+1 unit = thirteen fives or sixty-five)
```

Ask yourself what difficulties you had in doing the above and whether the explanations on each row helped in the understanding. Remember that children find base ten long multiplication just as confusing in the first instance. Similar explanations in base ten may help in the understanding of the structure of the system.

Russian Multiplication

There is a method of multiplication which only involves multiplication by two. It is given below not because it is a method which children ought to know but because it can be of interest and give pleasure to primary-school children. They should be encouraged to find out why the method works. The following examples are given so that the reader may (i) try to puzzle out the method and (ii) then find out why the method gives the correct results.

Example 1.

13× 14
~~6× 28~~
3× 56
1×112
———
182 i.e. 13×14 = 182.

Example 2.

25× 15
~~12× 30~~
~~6× 60~~
3×120
1×240
———
375 i.e. 25×15 = 375.

Example 3.

15× 25
7× 50
3×100
1×200
———
375 i.e. 15×25 = 375.

The following explanation should only be read when the reader has tried to puzzle out the method and the reason behind it.

Explanation

Method: (i) The numbers in the left-hand column are halved each time and the remainders discarded whilst the numbers in the right-hand column are doubled.

(ii) When a number in the left-hand column is even then the row is crossed out, when it is odd it is left in. The sum of the remaining numbers in the right-hand side is then found.

Reason Why the Method Gives the Correct Result

Consider first a simple example, namely 8×7. 8×7 can be replaced by 4×14; 4×14 can be replaced by 2×28; 2×28 can be replaced by 1×56. Thus it could be set out as follows:

~~8×7~~
~~4×14~~
~~2×28~~
1×56

56

Since each row has been replaced it is no longer needed and is crossed out.

Consider now the problem of finding 9×7.

9×7 cannot be replaced by 4×14 for 4 fourteens is only 8 sevens. Consequently an extra seven must be added in later. When the number is even the following row replaces the previous row and so the row is crossed out. When a number is odd the row is not replaced completely and so is not crossed out.

An interesting explanation is revealed when the problem is worked out using the binary notation.

Consider first the binary representation of Example 3 above.

In binary fifteen is represented by 1111 and twenty-five by 11001.

11001 ↔	twenty-five	
1111 ↔	fifteen	
11001 ↔	twenty-five	15× 25
110010 ↔	fifty	7× 50
1100100 ↔	one hundred	3×100
11001000 ↔	two hundred	1×200
101110111 ↔	three hundred and seventy-five	375

Now consider Example 2.

1111	↔ fifteen	
11001	↔ twenty-five	
1111	↔ fifteen	25× 15
00000	↔ zero not thirty hence crossed out	~~12× 30~~
000000	↔ zero not sixty hence crossed out	~~6× 60~~
1111000	↔ one hundred and twenty	3×120
11110000	↔ two hundred and forty	1×240
101110111	⟵⟶	375

Bicimals

Important

It is not the intention of the authors that primary-school children should be given any knowledge of bicimals. This section has been included for the benefit of the reader and not for children. It is hoped that a study of bicimals will help the student teacher to appreciate the difficulties children face when they meet decimals for the first time. It is further hoped that the explanations used to help the reader understand bicimals may be adapted by the student when teaching about decimals.

Reminder. In the base ten system ten units are replaced by one ten, ten tens by one hundred, ten hundreds by one thousand, etc. This relationship between the values of the various columns can be extended to the right of the units column and a decimal point is inserted merely to show where the units column is located. The attention of the child is often directed to the decimal point when it should be stressed that it is the units column which is the important feature and not the point. Thus one-tenth can be represented as 0·1 because ten-tenths can be replaced by one unit; one-hundredth by 0·01 because ten-hundredths can be replaced by one-tenth. It is tens relationship between the various columns which still applies.

Note. It is not helpful to instruct children that in the number 123·456, for example, the hundreds are *three* places to the left of the decimal point whilst the hundredths are *two* places to the right. It is very confusing to children who get mixed up between the "three and the two". It is much more helpful to explain that the hundreds column is located *two* columns to the left of the units column and the hundredths *two* columns to the right of the units column.

Q. 1. What would 0·1 and 0·01 mean if the notation was binary and not base ten? (It should be noted that these are called bicimals and not decimals.)

2. What do the binary numbers 111 and 0·111 represent?

3. Can you represent the fraction one-fifth as a bicimal?

A. 1. 0·1 means one-half and 0·01 means one-quarter.

2. 111 represents the number seven, i.e. 4+2+1, 0·111 represents one-half+one-quarter+one-eighth, i.e. four-eighths+two-eighths+one-eighth, i.e. seven-eighths.

(Remember that in decimals it is important to recognize 0·123 not only as one-tenth plus two-hundredths plus three-thousandths but also as one-hundred-and-twenty-three-thousandths. The reader should write down several bicimals and try to interpret them each in two ways as above.)

3. 0·0011001100110011......... or written as a recurring bicimal $0{\cdot}\dot{0}\dot{0}\dot{1}\dot{1}$.

Ask yourself (i) what were your difficulties in finding the solution to question 3 and (ii) whether you really understood what you were doing or whether you used an algorithm mechanically without thinking at each stage what you were writing. The following considerations may help you to understand more fully what is involved in recurring decimals and bicimals. Consider the problem of finding the decimal equivalent of one-third. The fraction one-third may have arisen as a result of trying to share a bar of chocolate equally between three people. Each person should receive one-third of the bar. However, when finding the decimal equivalent we have the restriction that the bar may only be cut into ten equal parts and any remaining pieces be cut into ten equal parts and so on. Each person could not get a whole bar so the whole unit is changed into ten-tenths. On sharing between three people each receives three-tenths and there is one-tenth left over. This is now changed into ten-hundredths each receiving three-hundredths with one-hundredth left over. The process can be continued indefinitely. We say that one-third can be expressed as a recurring decimal and written as either 0·33333333... or $0{\cdot}\dot{3}$. At a deeper level the problem is one dealing with limits of geometric progressions and the reader who wishes to consider this further should consult any textbook dealing with geometric progressions and the conditions for the existence of "sums to infinity".

Consider now a similar argument for finding the bicimal equivalent of one-fifth. Here the problem is that of sharing a whole unit equally between five people, the restriction being that we may only cut the unit into two equal parts, the parts into two equal parts and so on. Here again each person cannot get a whole unit. The unit is changed into two halves but as there are five people there is not even a half for each. Each half is changed into two quarters giving four quarters in all. Thus there is not even a quarter for each person. The next step is to change the four quarters into eight eighths and each person receives one-eighth with three-eighths left over.

Finally, the three-eighths are changed into six-sixteenths. Each person receives one-sixteenth with one-sixteenth left over. So far each person has received no halves, no quarters, one-eighth, and one-sixteenth, i.e. $0{\cdot}0+0{\cdot}00+0{\cdot}001+0{\cdot}0001$ or $0{\cdot}0011$ and there is one-sixteenth still to be shared. It is clear that the problem is now similar to that at the start of sharing one unit and the process continues in exactly the same way. Thus as a bicimal one-fifth will recur in cycles or blocks of four, i.e. $0{\cdot}001100110011\ldots$ or $0{\cdot}\dot{0}\dot{0}\dot{1}\dot{1}$.

Pattern in Other Bases

The use of pattern in number has already been stressed. Many such patterns in base ten have their counterparts in other bases and provide interesting puzzles as to why the patterns "work".

Example. In base ten the nine times table has the pattern that the digits have a sum nine as shown.

$$\begin{array}{ll} 1\times9 = 9 & \\ 2\times9 = 18 & 1+8 = 9 \\ 3\times9 = 27 & 2+7 = 9 \\ 4\times9 = 36 & 3+6 = 9\text{, etc.} \end{array}$$

In base five the four times table will have a similar pattern.

Thus:

$$1\times 4 = 4$$
$$2\times 4 = 13 \qquad 1+3 = 4$$
$$3\times 4 = 22 \qquad 2+2 = 4$$
$$4\times 4 = 31 \qquad 3+1 = 4.$$

Explain why the pattern is as it is. Does the pattern continue?

Q. In base ten there is a simple test to find out whether a number is divisible by nine or not. It consists of finding the sum of all the digits and testing whether this sum is divisible by nine or not. If it is then the original number is divisible by nine. If it is not then the number is not. Why is this test correct?

A. If a number is divisible by nine then the corresponding number of articles could be shared equally between nine people with no articles left over. Consider, for example, sharing 2574 articles between nine people.
When the 2000 articles are shared there are 2 left over.
(This is because $1000 = 999+1$ and hence $2000 = 2\times 999+2\times 1$.)
When the 500 articles are shared there are 5 left over.
(This is because $100 = 99+1$ and hence $500 = 5\times 99+5\times 1$.)
When 70 articles are shared there are 7 left over.
(This is because $10 = 9+1$ and hence $70 = 7\times 9+7\times 1$.)
When the 4 articles are shared there are 4 left over.
Hence when 2574, i.e. $2000+500+70+4$, articles are shared there will be $2+5+7+4$, i.e. 18 articles left over. These 18 can now be shared out equally and so 2574 is divisible by 9.
The argument used in this example can clearly be used and extended to cover all such examples.

Note. The pattern

$$10 = 9+1$$
$$100 = 99+1$$
$$1000 = 999+1$$
$$10000 = 9999+1$$

can clearly be extended indefinitely.

Q. Is there a simple test to find out whether a number is divisible by four in base five?

A. The test will be as in the previous example, e.g. 2141 base five is divisible by four since $2+1+4+1$, i.e. eight, is divisible by four.

As a long division in base five it may be set out as follows:

```
   244
4/2141
  13
  --
   34
   31
   --
    31
    31
    --
    ..
    --
```

If you find the above difficult to understand then you may be more aware of the difficulties that children experience when the long division algorithm is taught without any real understanding.

Example. Write down any number in base ten between 100 and 999. Repeat the same three digits in the same order to give a six-digit number. (Thus if the original number were 427 the six-digit number would be 427427.)

Divide this number by 13. Divide the quotient by 11. Finally divide the new quotient by 7. What do you notice about the result? Can you explain this?

In the example we have:

$$427427 \div 13 = 32879$$

$$32879 \div 11 = 2989$$

$$2989 \div 7 = 427.$$

The explanation can easily be found when it is realized that $13 \times 11 \times 7 = 1001$.

Can you make up similar examples in other bases?

Here is one in base five.

Write down a sensible three-digit number in base five (i.e. since base five is used only the symbols 0, 1, 2, 3, 4 may be used). Repeat the same three digits in the same order to get a six-digit number. Divide the number successively by seven, six and three as in the previous example. What do you notice? Can you explain this?

For example, if the base five number chosen had been 243 the result would be:

$$243243 \div 12 = 20224$$
$$20224 \div 11 = 1334$$
$$1334 \div 3 = 243.$$

(*Note*. In the above all numbers are in base five.)

CHAPTER 5

OPEN SENTENCES, NUMBER FACTS AND PICTORIAL REPRESENTATION

IN THE last chapter we considered in some detail the Hindu–Arabic system of recording and the use of bases other than ten in helping to understand the structure of that system. Before studying in detail the operations of addition, subtraction, multiplication and division it is necessary to develop the theme of Chapter 2 and to stress the importance of counting, number fact experiences and various methods of pictorial representation. The idea of an open sentence is helpful in this connection.

Open Sentence

Remember that the term universal set is used for the set of elements under consideration from which various subsets are chosen because of some relationship. Consider the universal set consisting of the following names of some counties:

{Staffordshire, Lancashire, Derbyshire, Lanarkshire, Perthshire}.

Consider also the open sentence:

... is a county of England.

This is called an open sentence because it is not complete as yet but contains a blank space. The blank space is now replaced by each of the members of the universal set in turn. Thus when the blank is replaced by "Staffordshire" we obtain the sentence: Staffordshire is a county of England. This statement is true.

When the blank is replaced by "Lanarkshire" the sentence becomes Lanarkshire is a county of England. This statement is false. The universal set can thus be partitioned into two subsets, one containing those members which make the statement true and the other containing those members which make the statement false. We are usually interested in the first of these two subsets which is called the truth set for the open sentence. A further example will help to make the idea clear.

Consider the universal set:

$$\{1.2.3.4.5.6.7.8.9\}$$

and the open sentence: $2+\square = 5.$

As each of the numbers 1, 2, 3, 4, 5, 6, 7, 8, 9 is used in place of the box, $\square$, we obtain statements which are either true or false. Clearly the only true statement is $2+3 = 5$. In this case the truth set is $\{3\}$, i.e. it is a set containing one element only. Considering the same universal set and the open sentence $2+\square > 5$ the truth set now contains six members and is:

$$\{4, 5, 6, 7, 8, 9\}.$$

Q. In each of the following questions the universal set is $\{1, 2, 3, 4, 5, 6, 7, 8, 9, 10, 11, 12, 13, 14, 15\}$. Find the truth sets for the following open sentences.
1. $6+\square = 14$, **2.** $6+\square < 14$,
3. $6+\square \leqslant 14$, **4.** $6+10 = \square$,
5. $\{\square | 2\times\square < 10\}$, **6.** $\{x | x \text{ is a prime number}\}$.

A. 1. $\{8\}$, **2.** $\{1, 2, 3, 4, 5, 6, 7\}$, **3.** $\{1, 2, 3, 4, 5, 6, 7, 8\}$,
4. $\{\ \}$ (The empty set since 16 is not included in the universal set.)
5. $\{1, 2, 3, 4\}$, **6.** $\{2, 3, 5, 7, 11, 13\}$

Children can be introduced to the idea of a truth set and use the language at an early age. For example, a 5-year-old child may be shown a picture of a cat sitting on a table. The open sentence might be: The cat is sitting ... the table. The universal set could then be {on, under, over}. Thus whilst the child is learning the correct vocabulary he can also be using the language which will be of use to him in mathematics.

Number Facts (Number Bonds)

The open sentence is particularly useful in helping children to learn number facts. At the end of Chapter 2 it was mentioned that children need to spend much time using conkers, shells, counters, toys and all kinds of material partitioning sets and recording discoveries. For example, a set of five toy cars may be partitioned into a subset containing two toys and another subset containing three toys. He may record this fact in several different ways.

For example, (i) by drawing a picture:

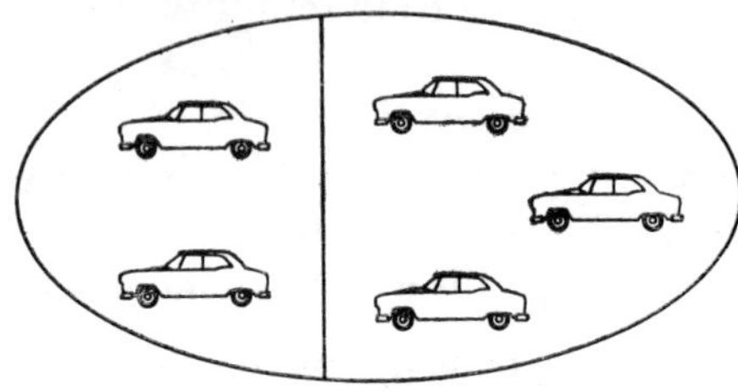

(ii) as an ordered pair mapped on to its image under the operation addition as either

$$(2, 3) \xrightarrow{\text{altogether}} 5$$

or

$$(2, 3) \xrightarrow{\text{add}} 5$$

or

$$(2, 3) \xrightarrow{+} 5$$

(iii) as $2+3 = 5$.

Note. (iii) will be read as "two plus three is another way of writing five". This is more meaningful than two and three equals five though this latter form may later be used.

It is essential that if a child is to become efficient at arithmetical calculations he should not only understand the structure of the Hindu–Arabic system but he must also know all the number facts for numbers to twenty and extend this knowledge to other numbers. It is important that he should not be rushed at too early a stage on to formal "tens and units calculations" but be given all kinds of material to help him discover and remember number facts and relationships. Experiences of weighing and measuring are essential. (Because of lack of space detailed considerations of measurement and practical work are not included in this volume but will be dealt with fully in Book 2.) Remember it is important that the teacher devises situations that will help the child to understand and remember these relationships. To say that a child really knows the 2, 3, 5 relationship implies that he knows:

$$2+3 = 5, \quad 3+2 = 5, \quad 5 = 2+3, \quad 5 = 3+2$$
$$5-3 = 2, \quad 5-2 = 3, \quad 2 = 5-3, \quad 3 = 5-2.$$

He must also be able to find the truth set for the following open sentences:

$\square+3 = 5$, $2+\square = 5$, $2+3 = \square$,

$3+\square = 5$, $\square+2 = 5$, $3+2 = \square$ and so on for each of the eight number facts listed above. (There are 32 in all.)

The 32 must not be taught as isolated facts but the child must come to realize that any one of these implies all the rest. If he is aware of the commutative property of addition, for example, he will know that if $3+4 = 7$ is true then so is $4+3 = 7$.

At a certain stage it will be helpful if the child records the number facts systematically. For example he might write the story of five. This would include:

$1+4 = 5$, $4+1 = 5$, $5 = 1+4$, $5 = 4+1$, $5-1 = 4$ and so on... $2+3 = 5$, $3+2 = 5$, etc.

Remember:

(i) The child abstracts from the concrete. Structural material should be available as long as necessary. (This includes shells, conkers, beads, etc., as well as commercially produced material.)

(ii) Do not force the material to be used when it is not needed.

(iii) Discussion is vital to make sure there is understanding and not just "parrot learning".

(iv) Practice is still necessary for efficiency but the aim should be to see how little practice is needed to maintain efficiency.

Counting

Counting forms the basis of much of the work in understanding and learning number facts. Suppose that a child wishes to find the truth set (sometimes also called the solution set) for the following open sentence:

$$3+4=\square.$$

He may put out a set of three shells and another set of four shells. He then places them in one larger set. To find out how many there are he may start counting one, two, three, four, five, six, seven, or at a later stage he may count on from three, i.e. merely count four, five, six, seven. (We have assumed that he is already clear about one-to-one correspondence.) This idea of counting on is most important. Thus at an early stage the teacher in discussion will bring out that five is one more than four and the idea of counting on is born. Counting back is just as important so that not only must it be stressed that five is one more than four but also that four is one less than five.

Counting in twos starting from zero is very important in helping to build up the two times table but the teacher should not forget that counting in twos *starting from any number* is just as important. It is also important to be able to count back as well as on. Thus time sometimes spent in mental work counting from any number either backwards or forwards in twos, threes, fours, tens, etc., is time well spent.

The Number Line

From an early age it is useful to represent numbers and number facts on a number line. The natural numbers can be represented geometrically in the following way.

Consider a starting-point *s*. A number of equal steps are made from this starting-point in a given direction. The points indicate the steps as shown.

•   •   •   •   •   •   •   •
S

The natural numbers are now inserted as shown:

S 1 2 3 4 5 6 7

The numeral 1 signifies that one step has been taken from the starting-point; the numeral 2 that two steps have been taken and so on. In order to ensure that the points are collinear it is advisable to draw a line segment thus:

Note. 1. At this stage we are only representing the natural numbers and so it is advisable to use *s* as the starting-point. Later on when the whole numbers are represented the *s* can be replaced by 0.

(The set of natural numbers is $\{1, 2, 3, 4, 5, 6, \ldots\}$.

The set of whole numbers is $\{0, 1, 2, 3, 4, 5, 6, 7, \ldots\}$.)

2. The arrow on the end of the line segment indicates that the line should be extended in one direction indefinitely.

3. There are no natural numbers between 1 and 2 or between 2 and 3, etc., so there is as yet no number represented between the points shown on the number line. At a later stage integers can be represented when the line has been extended to the left of the starting-point. Rational numbers can be represented by points in between those already shown and when finally the real numbers are introduced every point on the number line may be represented by a real number. (The development of number systems is considered fully in Book 2.)

With infants a number ladder should be used as well as a number line. Children can play games using dice or number spinners, moving toys made out of pipe cleaners up the ladder. The figure illustrates:

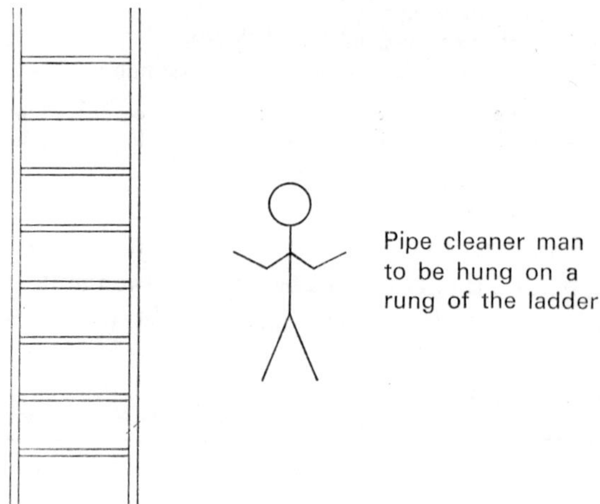

Addition can be illustrated on the number line as shown:

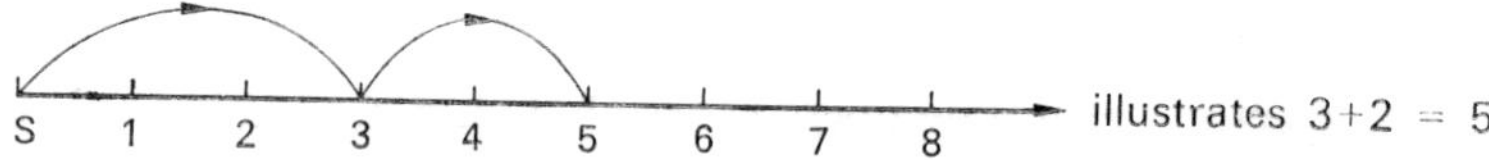

Subtraction can be illustrated also thus:

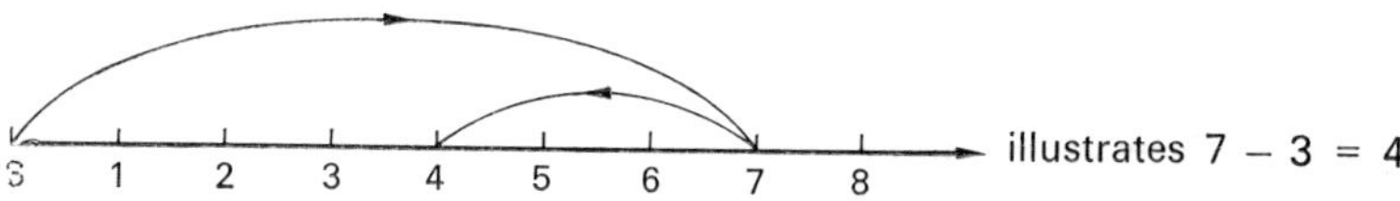

At a later stage sets of numbers may be graphed on number lines.

Examples.

Q. Graph the following sets on a number line.

(i) $\{4, 6, 8\}$.

(ii) $\{5, 7, 11, 13\}$.

(iii) The truth set for the open sentence $3+\square = 8$.
(iv) The truth set for the open sentence $3+\square < 8$.
The universal set for (iii) and (iv) is the set of natural numbers.

A. (i)

(ii)
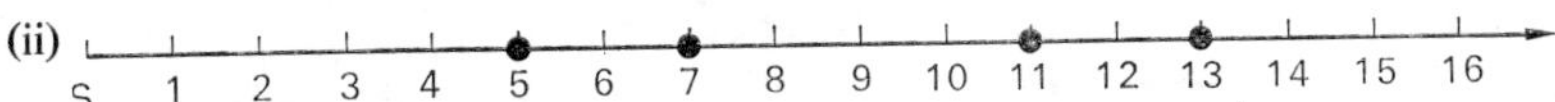

(iii)
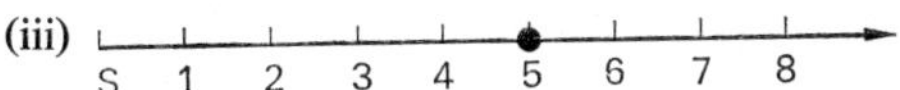

(iv)
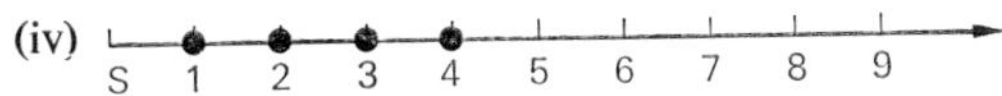

Instead of thickening the points as shown coloured pencils can be used to advantage.

The children should be encouraged to look for pattern whenever possible both on the one-dimensional graph and the sequence of numbers when shown as elements of a set. In the above (i) is the set of even numbers greater than 2 and less than 10 whilst (ii) is the set of prime numbers greater than 3 and less than 17. Top class Juniors can even express these two sets in set builder form.

Thus (i) is $\{x: x \text{ is an even number and } 2 < x < 10\}$,
(ii) is $\{y: 3 < y < 17 \text{ and } y \text{ is a prime number}\}$,
(iii) is $\{\square: 3+\square = 8 \text{ and } \square \text{ is a natural number}\}$,
and (iv) is $\{\square: 3+\square < 8 \text{ and } \square \text{ is a natural number}\}$.

If in (iii) and (iv) the universal set is changed to the set of real numbers the truth set for (iii) is not altered but that for four becomes an infinite set and the graph is:

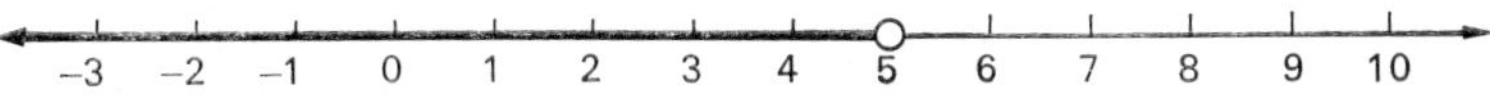

The discussion which goes hand in hand with the construction of these one-dimensional graphs is vital and prepares the way for two-dimensional graphs. (Two-dimensional graphs are considered fully in Book 2.)

The number line is not the only kind of pictorial representation which can help children to discover and understand more fully relationships of all kinds. Remember that mathematics deals with classifying and studying relationships and patterns of all kinds. Various methods of representing these relationships and of the aims behind pictorial representation are now considered.

Pictorial Representation

The following points should be borne in mind when using any form of pictorial representation.

(i) It is a simple way of representing relationships.

(ii) Less able children find it much easier to discover relationships when these are displayed in some pictorial fashion whilst the more able can develop the relationships further.

(iii) Pictorial representation provides situations for computation, discussion and further investigations.

(iv) It also provides writing situations.

Remember also

(i) If a graph or any kind of pictorial representation is drawn and then abandoned without discussion or without writing about it in some way and answering and making up questions about it then it has been a complete waste of time and is not worth drawing.

(ii) Children should be encouraged to present data in many varied ways and to discuss the advantages of the different methods. It is still true in this part of the work as it is in computation that it is better to do one thing in three ways than three things in one way or "one thing, many ways, sometimes!"

(iii) Children must write about their graphs on a separate piece of paper (often referred to as "the white paper"). They must also answer questions set by the teacher and make up questions which can be answered by studying the graphs.

Collection of Data

The first requisite for pictorial representation is that there must be data to represent. This must be something in which the children are interested and within their experience. Examples will often arise naturally out of classroom activities. At other times situations must be contrived and from the resultant discussion opportunity for various ways of presenting the data will develop. For example, a class of 6- or 7-year-olds were discussing pets. The question arose as to which pet they preferred. The following are ways of representing this material.

Mapping

Two large circles were drawn and in one pictures of various pets placed. Each child had also a piece of sticky paper on which he wrote his name. These were stuck in the other circle and pieces of wool joined the names to the appropriate pet. The relation for the mapping was "the pet I like best is". The figure shows only some of the names.

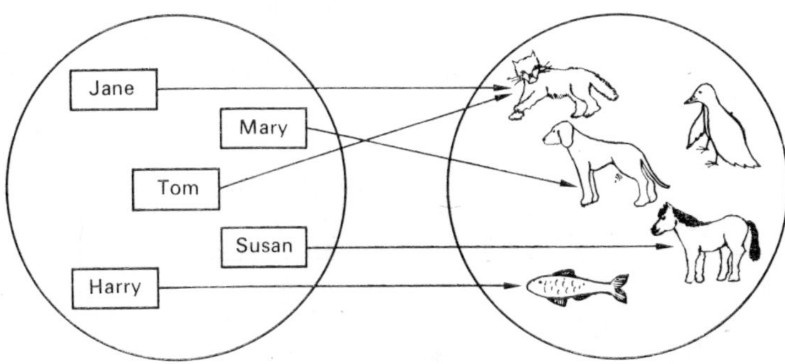

The pet I like best is

Note. There are two sets, a set of children's names and a set of the names of pets. This is called a mapping since each member of the first set is mapped on to a *unique* member of the second set. For a mapping *every* member of the first set must have one and only one *image* in the second set.

Had the circles been drawn as in the next figure the relation would have been "is the favourite pet of".

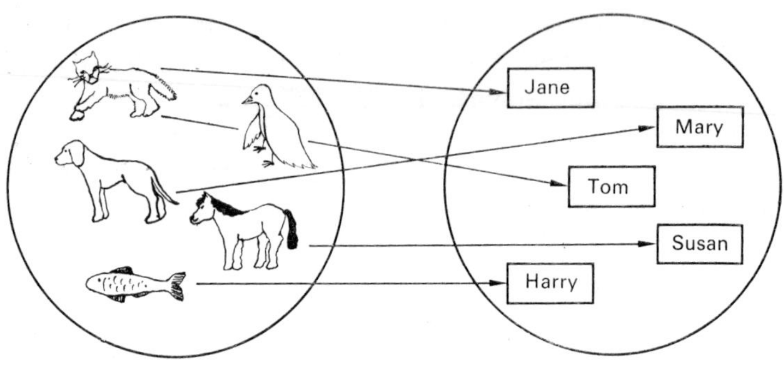

This would not have been a mapping although some books do call it a mapping. It is better to refer to it as a relation. Some of the elements of the first set have more than one image and the bird has no image. A mapping is a special kind of relation which satisfies the condition already stated above.

Q. Which of the following diagrams represent a mapping?

(i)

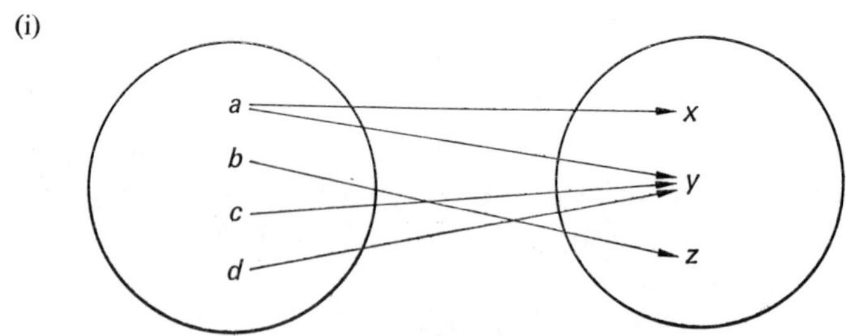

(ii)

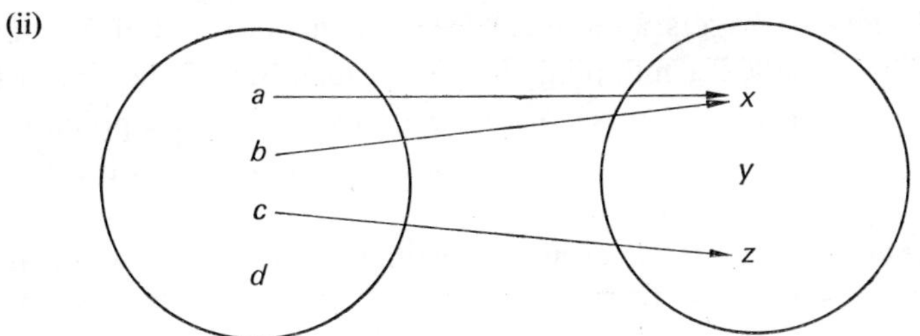

(iii)

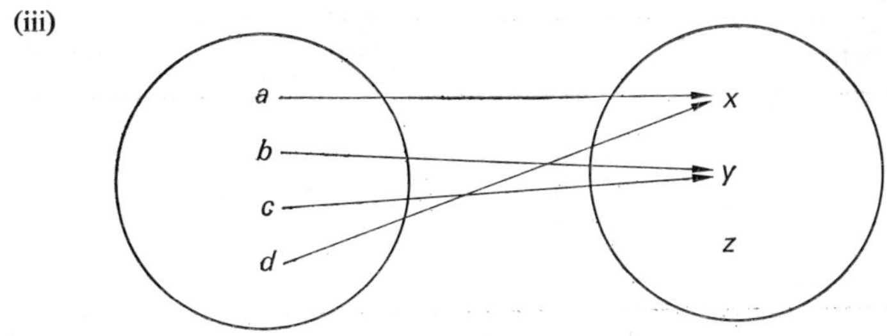

A. Only (iii) is a mapping. In (i) the member *a* has two images and in (ii) *d* has no image.

Q. In the mapping "the pet I like best is" what would you do with it when the children had made the diagrams?

A. (i) There would have been discussion.

(ii) The children would have written a story about it describing what they did.

(iii) Questions would be set such as: Which pet was liked by most children? How many more children liked dogs than cats, etc.?

(iv) The children would have made up questions about the graph.

There could have been several minor changes in the drawing of the mapping. For example, instead of pieces of wool, lines could have been drawn; names of the pets instead of pictures could have been used.

Instead of representing as a mapping the data could have been shown on a chart or on a lattice or as a partition of a set.

Chart

	Cat	Dog	Goldfish	Pony	Bird
Jane	×				
Mary		×			
Tom	×				
Susan				×	
Harry			×		

Lattice

Either:

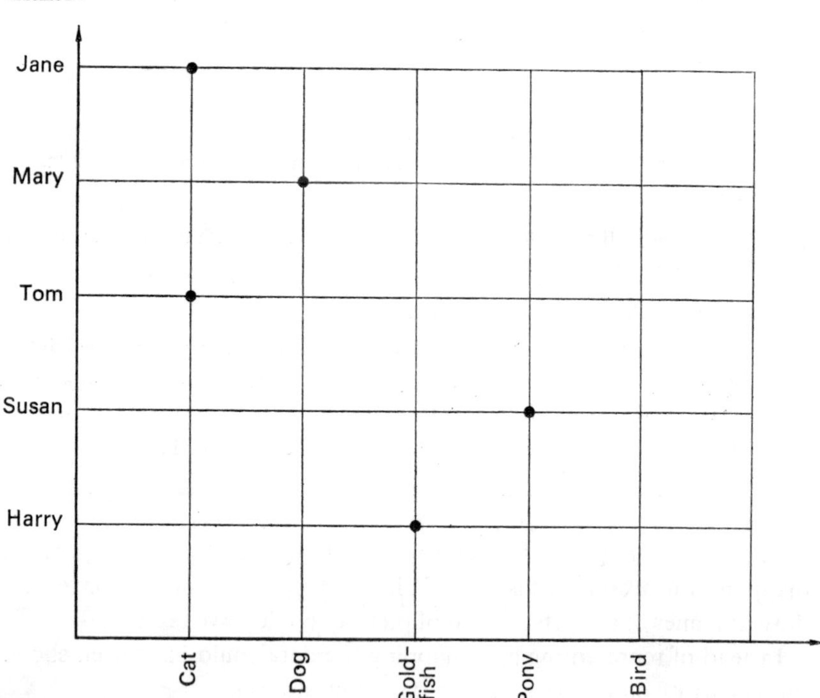

Or:

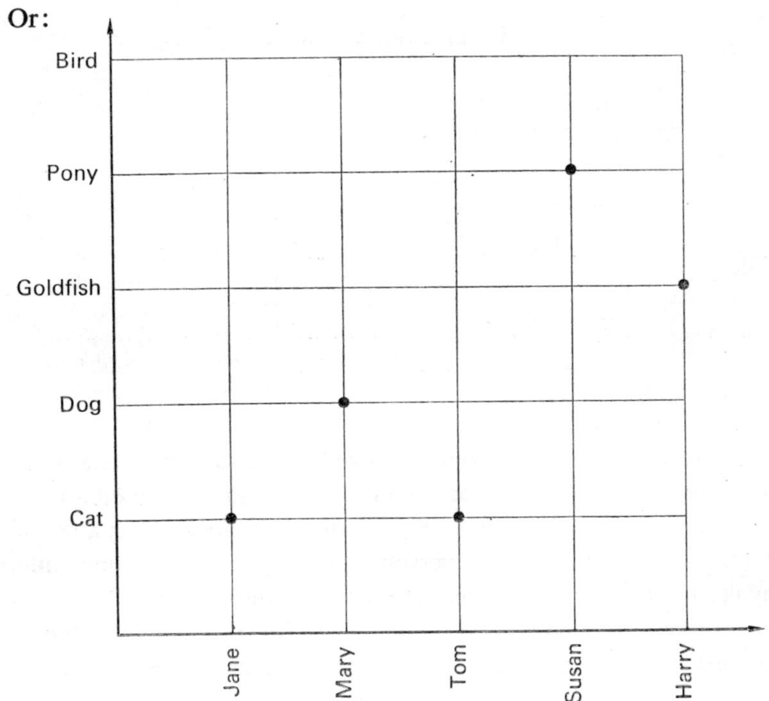

Partition of a Set of Names

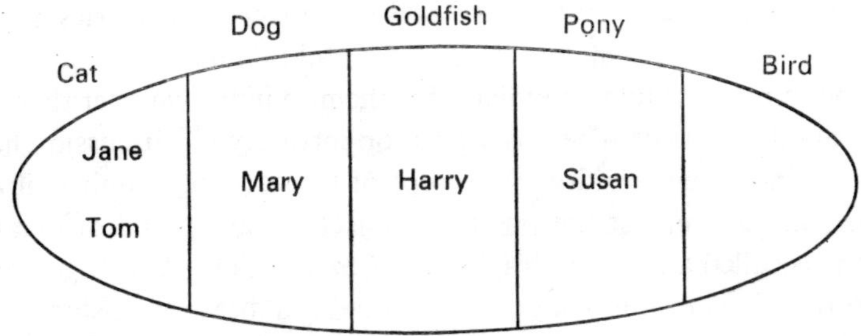

The information could also be shown in a form leading to block graphs and bar charts.

Various Block Graphs

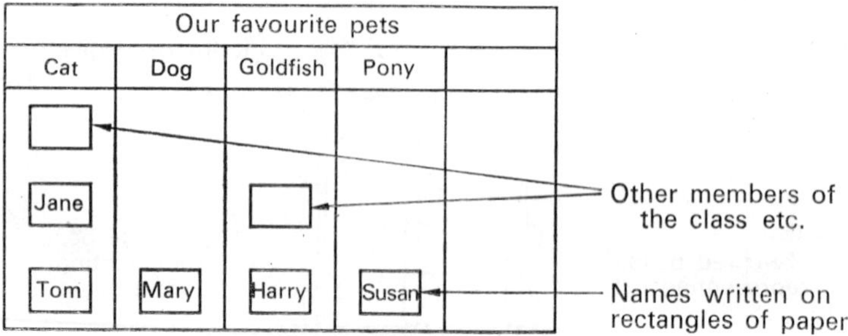

The same picture might be drawn horizontally instead of vertically.

In the examples that have been considered so far a name on a piece of paper has represented a person. Eventually on a block graph a coloured square will represent either a person or an object. Very young children may need to have concrete objects to represent the elements of the set and then progress at a later stage to the more abstract coloured block or coloured square. For example, if children become interested in a traffic census the youngest children would probably bring toy cars, lorries, etc., to represent the traffic. These toys would be laid out in rows or columns. Slightly older children might have pictures of cars, lorries, etc., which they can stick in rows on paper. In either case it is probable that the lorries would occupy more space than the cars and a row of six lorries might be longer than a row of ten cars. Unless the children match the lorries and cars one to one it would be difficult for them to judge whether there were more cars than lorries. There is a great opportunity for discussion here, a check on individual children's concept of the cardinal number of a set. Incidentally the representation of the objects by some kind of picture in this way is called an *isotype* graph or a *pictogram*. The next stage towards the abstract idea of a block graph is probably a three-dimensional representation. In the traffic-census example a car might be represented by a cotton reel, a bead, a unifix block or cardboard box. The following diagrams illustrate these ideas.

1. Knitting needles can be fastened into plasticine and coloured beads put on to the needles, red for cars, green for lorries, blue for buses and so on.

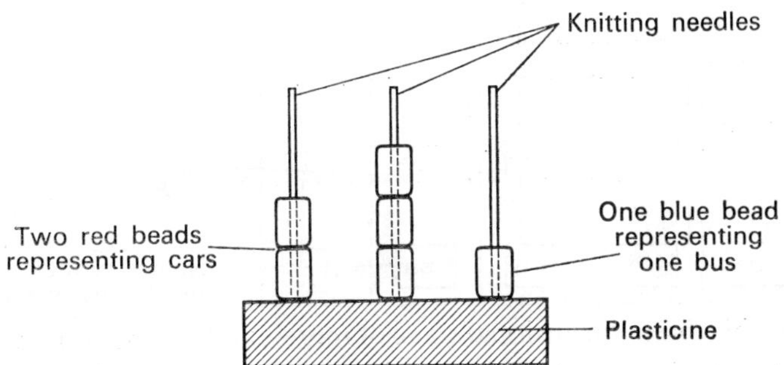

2. Dowel rods may be fastened into a block of wood and cotton reels or beads placed on the rods.

3. Beads may be threaded on to string and the strings hung as shown.

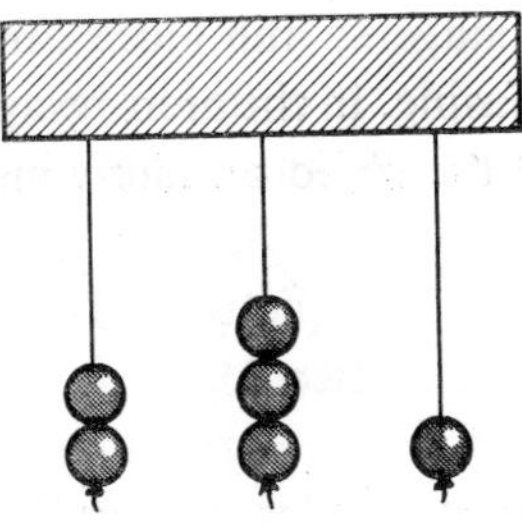

4. Coloured blocks of unifix may be fastened together and placed in rows or columns.

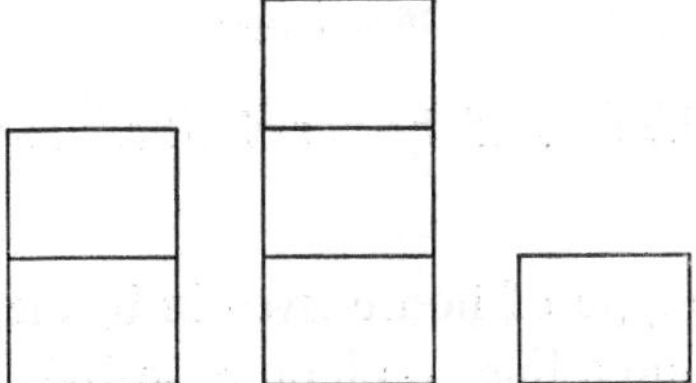

5. Match boxes may be placed in rows.

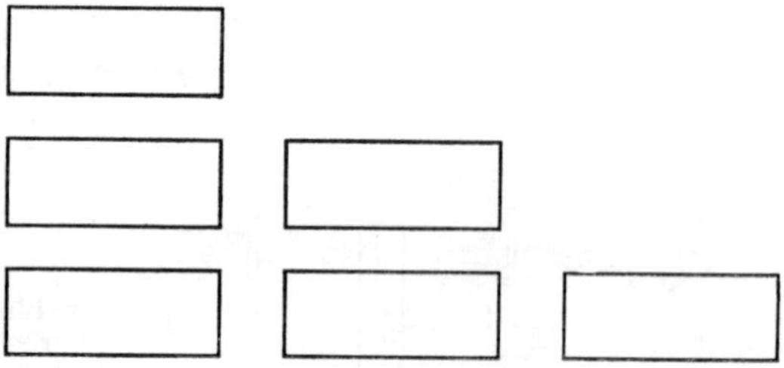

After this three-dimensional stage of representation the children should be able to understand the abstract ideas of a block graph, bar chart or line graph.

Block Graph

It is advisable to use squared paper where the squares have centimetre sides. Graph paper divided into millimetres may be used but the very small squares can be confusing. In the block graph each square is coloured in some way to represent the objects under consideration.

Bar Chart

The bar chart differs from the block graph only in that in the bar chart the squares are joined together into one large rectangle in each column.

Line Graph

In the line graph the bars of the bar chart are replaced by singles lines as shown.

A bar chart of the type of house lived in by the children in a class is shown on page 107 and a line graph on page 108.

Number of houses
15
14
13
12
11
10
9
8
7
6
5
4
3
2
1
Terraced
Semi-detached
Detached
Bungalow
Caravan

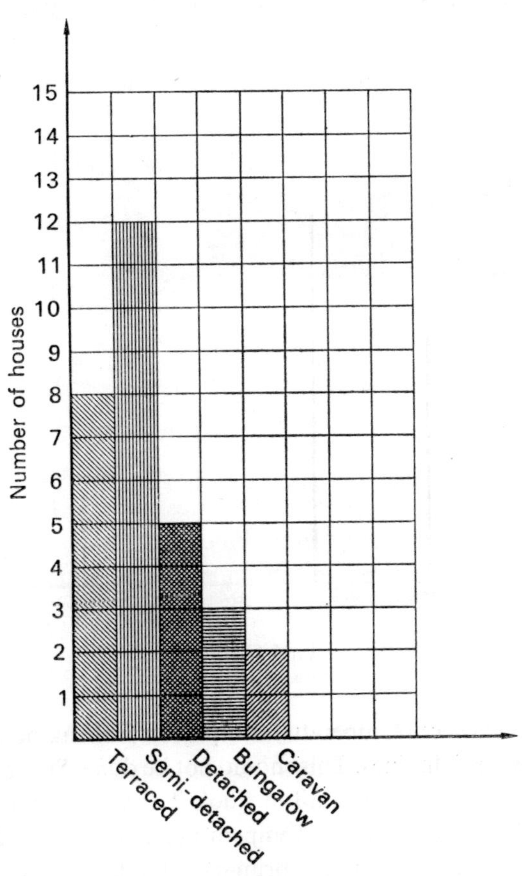

BAR CHART

Remember. 1. In answering questions on block graphs, bar charts and line graphs the children should be encouraged to interpret from the graph and not from the original statistics.

2. Do not join the tops of the columns in a line graph. This has no meaning.

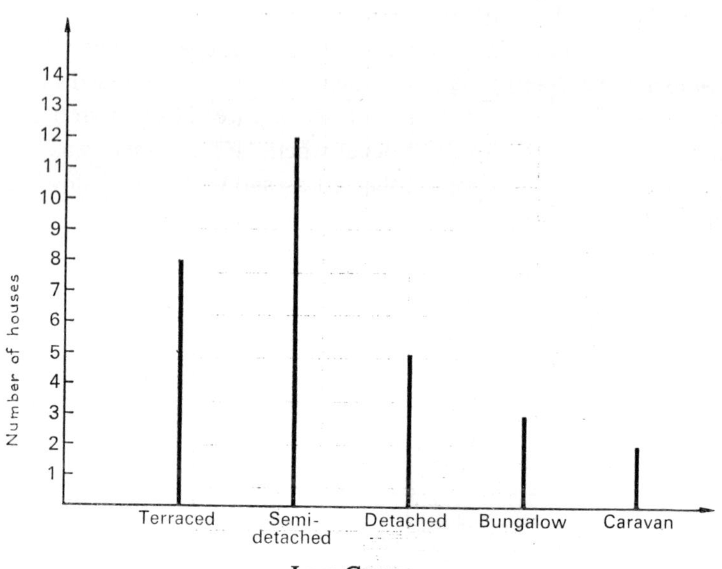

LINE GRAPH

3. Some books show temperature graphs by plotting points which are then joined by straight lines. This should not be done. Straight line graphs will be considered in more detail in Book 2 and the question of joining points will also be dealt with. Temperature graphs should be done as block graphs or bar charts in the primary school.

4. Many books wrongly refer to bar charts as histograms. In a histogram the area under the graph and not the height of the bar is the important consideration. Histograms are used in statistics when dealing with frequency distributions. It is unlikely that many histograms will be drawn in the primary school.

5. Children should be interested in the data which they represent and should collect it before they draw the graphs. Often it is possible to collect the data in a systematic way by using a tally chart as follows.

Tally Chart

After some preliminary discussion with a teacher, top-class Juniors became interested in probability and the laws of chance. They wanted to find out what was likely to happen when four coins were tossed simultaneously and to discover how often four heads, three heads, two heads, one head and no heads were likely to occur when the experiment was repeated many times. The results were collected as shown in the following tally chart.

Four heads	|	1
Three heads	~~||||~~ |	6
Two heads	~~||||~~ ~~||||~~	10
One head	~~||||~~	5
No heads	||	2

When the four coins were tossed first there were two heads and two tails. A stroke was then put as shown opposite the row "two heads". The experiment was repeated and corresponding strokes made. Notice that the fifth stroke in any row is drawn obliquely to facilitate counting. The four coins were tossed simultaneously twenty-four times in all. The results could be represented by drawing either a block graph, bar chart or line graph. In this case too since 360 is easily divisible by 24 they could be shown on a Pi graph as follows.

Pi Graph

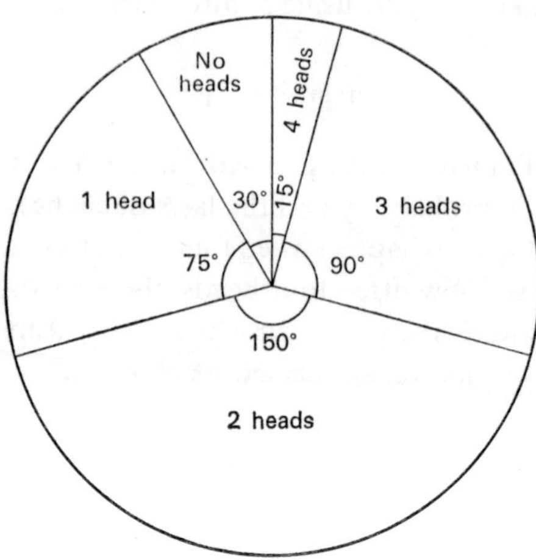

The Pi graph should only be used when the children are able to use a protractor and when the total number of objects to be represented is a simple factor of 360. It is perhaps more appropriate for the secondary-school child than the primary.

CHAPTER 6

NATURAL NUMBERS AND ADDITION

THE natural numbers are those we use when we make a count of the elements of any set. This counting is a mapping operation in which one set of objects is placed in one-to-one correspondence with another set. The sets, (a ball, a bat, a wicket), (Tom, Dick, Harry), (a bicycle, a car, a bus), have one property in common, which is the fact that they can be mapped one-to-one exactly. They are equivalent sets. This property is defined by the number of elements in each set, and such a number is called a *cardinal number*. Sets can be arranged by their cardinality. The cardinal numbers obtained in this way are called the counting numbers, but for mathematical purposes they are called the set of natural numbers, and are represented by the numerals $\{1, 2, 3, 4, \ldots\}$.

The condition governing this set of natural numbers is that each element represents a class of equivalent sets. It is through experiences of three pens, three dolls, three cars and so on that a child eventually understands the abstract notion of three. The difficulty about number is that it is abstract and therefore not easy to illustrate. It is quite easy to produce a set of three objects, but to point out this set is not to point out the *number three*. We record how many elements this set contains by writing a numeral, 3. We are not pointing out the *number* 3, for only after vast experience of equivalent sets of three objects does the *abstract idea* of a whole class of three, that is, "threeness", become part of a person's abstract thought of number. As an analogy the idea of "blueness" only becomes part of us after many experiences of objects which we describe as "blue". An outstanding property of the natural numbers might be described as size, resulting in a definite order. This means that there is a first number, 1, and that each number has one, and only one, definite successor and so the set is an infinite series. We record like this:

Natural numbers $\{1, 2, 3, 4, 5, \ldots\}$

Fundamental Operations for Natural Numbers

Addition

The union of two sets A and B will be a set which contains either the members of set A or B or both set A and B.

$$A = \{3. 4. 5. 6\} \qquad B = \{6. 7. 8\}$$
$$A \cup B = \{3, 4, 5, 6, 7, 8\}$$
$$n(A) = 4$$
$$n(B) = 3$$
$$n(A \cup B) = 6$$

We observe $4+3 \neq 6$. The element 6 is a member of both sets and is counted twice when the sets are numerated separately but once when considering the union of the sets.

Study these examples.

$$A = \{3, 4, 5, 6\} \qquad B = \{4, 5, 6\}$$
$$A \cup B = \{3, 4, 5, 6\}$$
$$n(A) = 4$$
$$n(B) = 3$$
$$n(A \cup B) = 4 \quad \text{but} \quad 4+3 \neq 4$$

The sets are not disjoint. There are common members, $\{4, 5, 6\}$.

$$A = \{3, 4, 5, 6\} \qquad B = \{5, 6\}$$
$$A \cup B = \{3, 4, 5, 6\}$$
$$n(A) = 4$$
$$n(B) = 2$$
$$n(A \cup B) = 4 \quad \text{but} \quad 4+2 \neq 4$$

The sets are *not* disjoint. There are common members, $\{5, 6\}$.

$$A = \{3, 4, 5, 6\} \qquad B = \{7, 8\}$$

$$A \cup B = \{3, 4, 5, 6, 7, 8\}$$

$$n(A) = 4$$

$$n(B) = 2$$

$$n(A \cap B) = 6 \quad \text{and} \quad 4+2 = 6$$

The sets *are* disjoint. There are no common members.

If we consider defining addition in terms of the union of sets we can only do this if the members of the sets are non-overlapping. There must be no common members, the intersection of the sets is an empty set. When we meet sets which have no common members we refer to the sets as disjoint. Thesefore, addition can be defined as the union of disjoint sets or sets which have no common members.

The cardinal number of the union of disjoint sets will be the sum of the cardinal numbers of each set.

Given any two natural numbers, we can add them, the solution being known as the sum of the two natural numbers. If a and b are natural numbers, then there is *one* and *only one* natural number that we can call the sum of a and b and we record this sum as $a+b$.

The intuitive interpretation we give to addition of natural numbers *is based on counting*. Whenever we add, we are counting on, but our memories keep certain results at our finger tips and we know, at sight, what the results will be. These "finger-tip" results are known as number facts. When counting we use the set of numbers of the ordered sequence of natural numbers.

Set (3) (a set having 3 members):

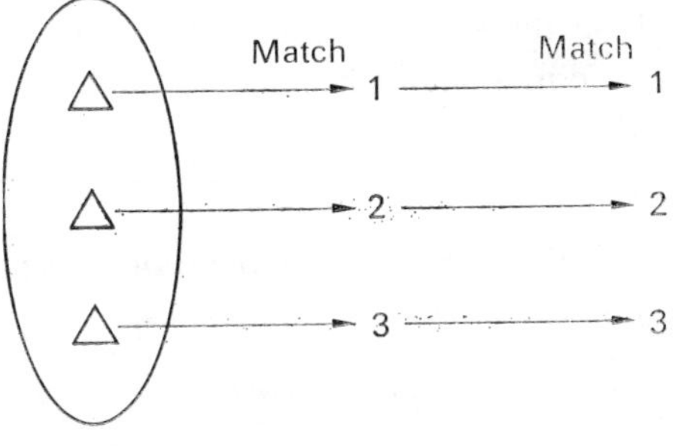

Set (4) (a set having 4 members and no intersection with set (3)):

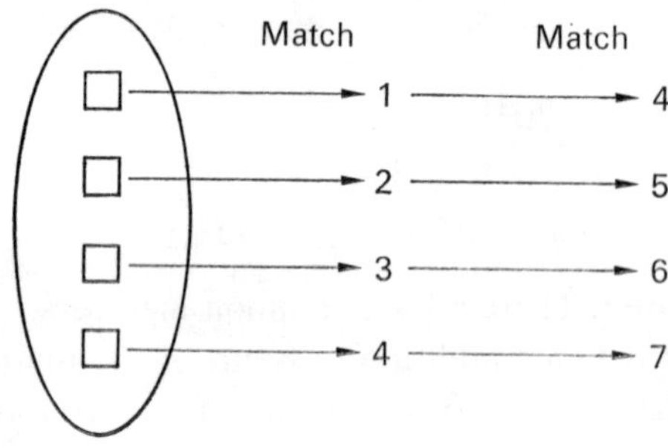

$$n\,\text{set}\,(3) = 3$$

$$n\,\text{set}\,(4) = 4$$

$$n\,(\text{set}\,(3) \cup \text{set}\,(4)) = 7$$

This idea is the basis of our number facts.

We know addition as an operation, and we are considering this operation using the set of natural numbers. How do we define an operation?

Essential Property of an Operation

The essential property of an *operation* is the UNIQUENESS of its result. We have described addition as *an operation*. This means that for any pair of natural numbers, say a and b, the *sum* is UNIQUE. There is no doubt about the result—there is ONE sum $(a+b)$ only.

We must never have ambiguous results.

$$(3, 5) \xrightarrow{\text{add}} 8. \textit{ The result } 8 \textit{ is unique}$$

Multiplication is an operation because the product of two natural numbers is UNIQUE.

$$(3, 5) \xrightarrow{\text{multiply}} 15 \quad \textit{The result } 15 \textit{ is unique}$$

Any relation which associates a unique number with each ordered pair of natural numbers is called an operation.

$$(1, 2) \rightarrow 4$$
$$(3, 4) \rightarrow 10$$
$$(4, 5) \rightarrow 13$$
$$(5, 6) \rightarrow 16$$

Here a unique natural number is associated with an ordered pair of numbers. They are *ordered*, because *with this relationship* it makes a difference to the unique result which member of the ordered pair is recorded first, and which second.

Look for the pattern in the relations above and you will soon discover a rule for associating a unique natural number with each ordered pair of natural numbers. In this example you may say "Double the first member of the pair, then add the second to the result".

You can define the operation (called an operation because of the unique number associated with each ordered pair) this way:

$$1 \text{ o } 2 \rightarrow 4$$
$$3 \text{ o } 4 \rightarrow 10$$
$$4 \text{ o } 5 \rightarrow 13$$
$$5 \text{ o } 6 \rightarrow 16$$

(o is the symbol for an operation)

The operation, o, is defined as, "For any natural numbers a and b,

$a \text{ o } b \rightarrow 2a+b$" (read "$a$ operation b gives $2a+b$")

Q. $(3, 4) \rightarrow 15$
using o to represent an operation,
$(5, 6) \rightarrow 23$
define o from these ordered pairs
$(7, 8) \rightarrow 31$
and their unique solutions.
$(8, 9) \rightarrow 35$

A. $a \text{ o } b = a+3b$

You can use symbols such as *, o, † to be operation symbols and they serve in the same way as "×" or "." serves for multiplication.

Special Properties under Addition

The set of natural numbers form an infinite series. You cannot come to an end when counting them, also, the whole is no greater than some of its parts. There are as many even natural numbers as there are natural numbers. If you name any natural number, you have only to add 1, and you have the next greater natural number. Yet we can visualize the set of natural numbers, even from

$$\{1, 2, 3, 4, 5, \ldots\ldots\ldots\ldots\ldots\}$$

If we *add* two natural numbers, the sum is also *in the set of natural numbers.*

$$3+5 = 8$$

3, 5 and 8 are natural numbers: the sum of 3 and 5 (both natural numbers) is 8 (also a natural number).

We say the set of natural numbers is *closed under addition.* Remember this means, "Add two natural numbers and the sum is also in the set of natural numbers". You will have heard of a "closed shop".

$$\{1, 2, 3, 4, 5 \ldots\ldots\ldots\ldots\ldots\ldots\}$$

(Natural number add natural number)→a member of set of natural numbers.

$$100+201 = 301$$

$$1760+220 = 1980$$

Q. Is the set of natural numbers closed under multiplication?

$$3\times4 = 12$$
$$880\times5 = 4400$$

Explain your conclusions.

A. The set of natural numbers is closed under multiplication. This means, for any two numbers, a and b, in the set of natural numbers, their product is also a member of the set of natural numbers. (Since we can express a multiplication situation in terms of repeated addition, we should expect this result.)

A set is closed under any operation if the result of performing the operation is also a member of the set.

Consider

$\{1, 2, 3, 4, 5, 6 \ldots\ldots\ldots\ldots\ldots\ldots\}$

$2+19 =$	Is the result a member
$3\times 18 =$	of the set of natural
$4-2 =$	numbers?
$2-4 =$	
$8\div 4 =$	
$4\div 8 =$	

Q. Is the set of natural numbers *always closed* under the operations of (i) addition, (ii) subtraction, (iii) multiplication, (iv) division? Test out some examples of your own.

A. (i) Yes. (ii) No. (iii) Yes. (iv) No.

Q. If "x o y" *represents* x, can o represent an operation in natural numbers? Is the set of natural numbers closed under the operation?

A. Let o represent the operation multiplication, and we are considering the set of natural numbers.

If x o $y \rightarrow x$ then y will be represented by the numeral 1, e.g. $3\times 1 = 3$, $170\times 1 = 170$. The set of natural numbers is closed under multiplication.

Note. If o represented the operation addition, and x o $y \rightarrow x$, then y would be represented by 0 which is *not* in the set of natural numbers.

$\{1, 2, 3, 4 \ldots\ldots\ldots\}$ The set of natural numbers.

$\{0, 1, 2, 3, 4 \ldots\ldots\ldots\}$ The set of whole numbers.

When we introduce 0 to the natural numbers, we refer to (0, 1, 2, 3, 4...) as the set of *whole* numbers NOT the set of natural numbers. So x o $y \rightarrow x$ is a closed operation if we are considering the set of *whole numbers*.

The Commutative Property

The *order* in which two natural numbers are considered does not affect the result when we are considering the operation of addition. For any NATURAL NUMBERS, a and b, we have $a+b = b+a$.

(a) $2+3 = 3+2$ (b) $A = (a, b) \quad B = \{c, d\}$

$2\times 3 = 3\times 2$ $A \cup B = \{a, b, c, d\}$

$B \cup A = \{a, b, c, d\}$

This all seems so trivial that we may ask if this property is worth thinking about?

Study these examples:

$$5+7 = 7+5$$

$$7-6 \neq 6-7 \quad (\neq \text{ means "is not equal to"})$$

$$8 \div 2 \neq 2 \div 8$$

The *order* of *adding* two numbers does not matter. Note that it does matter with some operations. Which?

$$5+7 = 7+5$$

(5+7) is another way of writing (7+5) because they are both ways of recording 12

OR

(5+7) designates the same number (12) as 7+5

(Here we are translating into longhand the symbol =.)

This important property is known as THE COMMUTATIVE PROPERTY OF ADDITION *for natural numbers.*

From the examples above, it is evident that subtraction and division do NOT possess this commutative property. We must always look for counter examples to any property discovered by the pupil. They must realize *all* operations are not commutative. Because multiplication possesses the commutative property a child has often eased his burden of "tables" learning in no uncertain manner. That (7×8) and (8×7) are ways of designating the same number, 56, has given comfort to many a pupil finding difficulty in memorizing "tables".

The Associative Property

We can add only two numbers at a time, so if we wish to find the sum of three, four, ten or any number, we must group, successively, into pairs.

Example:

$$5+6+7$$

We can add only in pairs—addition is a binary operation—so we say $(5+6) = 11$ and $(11+7) = 18$, i.e. $(5+6)+7$.

If we wished, we would say,

$$(6+7) = 13 \quad \text{and} \quad (5+13) = 18, \quad \text{i.e. } 5+(6+7)$$

Study this example. We have been dealing with

$$5+(6+7) \quad \text{and} \quad (5+6)+7$$

What is involved in obtaining this recording?

$$(5+7)+6$$

We start with

$$5+6+7$$

We associate 6 and 7, i.e. $5+(6+7)$.

Using the commutative property, we have $5+(7+6)$.

Using the associative property, we have $(5+7)+6$.

The manner of associating the numbers into pairs for adding and multiplying will not affect the final UNIQUE solution.

We may state,

FOR ANY NATURAL NUMBERS a, b and c,

$$a+(b+c) = (a+b)+c$$
$$3+(4+5) = (3+4)+5$$

The property of associating pairs when adding and not affecting the unique result is known as THE ASSOCIATIVE PROPERTY OF ADDITION for natural numbers.

Study these examples:

$$3\times(4\times5) = (3\times4)\times5$$

$$3+(4+5) = (3+4)+5$$

$$6-(5-4) \neq (6-5)-4$$

$$12 \div (4\div2) \neq (12 \div 4) \div 2$$

The associative property is satisfied with the operations of addition and multiplication but *not* with the operations of subtraction and division.

Thus $7-4-2$ is ambiguous. You cannot associate the numbers into pairs as you wish. You must use brackets to clarify your requirements.

(a) $3+4+5$ No brackets required for clarity.

(b) $3\times4\times5$ No brackets required for clarity.

(c) $7-4-2$ Brackets required.

(d) $12 \div 4 \div 2$ Brackets required.

Statements like (c) and (d) must not be written on the blackboard. They are ambiguous. You require brackets to give sense to the statements, e.g.

$$7-(4-2) \quad \text{or} \quad (7-4)-2$$

$$12 \div (4 \div 2) \quad \text{or} \quad (12 \div 4) \div 2$$

Because the operation of addition has the associative property (for natural numbers) *brackets are not essential*.

If ASSOCIATIVE PROPERTY No brackets required

If NON-ASSOCIATIVE Brackets required

Sometimes the commutative property for addition is referred to as the ORDER PRINCIPLE; and the associative property for addition as the GROUPING PRINCIPLE.

We will consider application of these properties to the classroom situation. Study these examples:

$$\begin{array}{ll} 7+8 = 7+(3+5) & 53+87 = 53+(47+40) \\ (7+3)+5 & (53+47)+40 \\ 10+5 & 100+40 \\ 15 & 140 \end{array}$$

The associative property or grouping principle motivates this development. Here is another example:

$$\begin{array}{ll} 27+(73+89) & 50+(50+49) \\ (27+73)+89 & (50+50)+49 \\ 100+89 & 100+49 \\ 189 & 149 \end{array}$$

Using the grouping principle simplifies the computation.

Q. Use the grouping principle (associative property) to simplify these addition problems.

(a) $(8+4)+6$ (b) $34+(6+9)$

(c) $(54+60)+40$ (d) $26+(74+23)$

(e) $(596+600)+400$ (f) $1500+(500+600)$

A. (a) $8+(4+6)$ (b) $(34+6)+9$ (c) $54+(60+40)$

(d) $(26+74)+23$ (e) $596+(600+400)$ (f) $(1500+500)+600$

Example:

Q. Rearrange $a+(b+c)$ to form $b+(a+c)$. Which principles or properties are you applying?

THIS IS ONE SOLUTION

$a+(b+c) \rightarrow (a+b)+c$ Grouping principle (Associativity)

then $(a+b)+c \rightarrow (b+a)+c$ Order principle (Commutativity)

and $(b+a)+c \rightarrow b+(a+c)$ Grouping principle (Associativity)

Rearranging $a+(b+c)$ to form $b+(a+c)$, we have used the associative property of addition, followed by the commutative property of addition, followed by the associative property of addition.

Q. Establish the following, giving reasons for your steps:

(i) $a+(b+c) = c+(a+b)$,
(ii) $a+(b+c) = b+(c+a)$.

A. (i) $a+(b+c) = a+(c+b)$ Commutative property of addition
$(a+c)+b$ Associative property of addition
$(c+a)+b$ Commutative property of addition
$c+(a+b)$ Associative property of addition.

(ii) $a+(b+c) = (a+b)+c$ Associative property of addition
$(b+a)+c$ Commutative property of addition
$b+(a+c)$ Associative property of addition
$b+(c+a)$ Commutative property of addition.

You may try other arrangements.

Q. (3 o 4) o 5 = 3 o (4 o 5). If o designates an operation, which operations would satisfy the statement above?

A. (i) Addition. (ii) Multiplication.
The statement informs us that the associative property is applicable and this property applies only to the operations of addition and multiplication.

Summary

Fundamental properties for natural numbers

1. Closure

The sum of any pair of natural numbers is a natural number. We say that the set of natural numbers is CLOSED under addition, e.g. $3+4 = 7$ and 3, 4 and 7 are natural numbers.

2. The commutative property

The ORDER of adding two natural numbers is not important.

We refer to the commutative property of natural numbers under addition.

$$2+5 = 5+2 \quad \text{but} \quad 7-4 \neq 4-7$$
$$\text{and} \quad 18 \div 6 \neq 6 \div 18$$

3. The associative property

Associating natural numbers into pairs when more than two numbers are involved in an operation does not affect the result.

We refer to the associative property of natural numbers under addition.

If an operation possesses the associative property, brackets are *not* required to clarify the situation.

$$3+(5+6) = (3+5)+6 \quad \text{but} \quad 18 \div (6 \div 3) \neq (18 \div 6) \div 3$$
$$\text{and} \quad 9-(5-4) \neq (9-5)-4$$

Zero

Reference has been made to the set of natural numbers and the set of whole numbers.

$$N = \{1, 2, 3, 4 \ldots\ldots\ldots\}$$
$$W = \{0, 1, 2, 3, 4 \ \ldots\ldots\}$$

The only difference is that the set of whole numbers contains one more element, zero.

The property of zero demonstrated here is

$$x+0 = x, \quad 0+x = x, \quad \text{for all values of} \quad x.$$

Add zero to any number and the number remains the same value.

$$5+0 \text{ or } 0+5 = 5$$

0 is referred to as *the additive identity element* and is of great value, later on.

N.B. The need to carry out any operation should arise from a situation which is real to the child. In the early stages, 19+14 or $\begin{array}{r}19\\+14\end{array}$ should not appear on the blackboard unless these quantities have arisen from an everyday situation.

$\begin{array}{r}19\\+14\\\hline\end{array}$ This recording, as it stands, is meaningless.

If we say, "19 boys and 14 girls from a class are going on a trip to the Zoo, how many less dinners will be required at school on that day?", then the child sees a purpose in carrying out the addition.

We begin our survey of addition from a computational viewpoint by considering briefly counting and place value.

Counting Experience

We have discussed the set of natural numbers and their properties. For many years the pupil will be discovering methods of computation, using only this set of natural numbers. We are going to consider preparatory experiences leading to the understanding of the operations of addition, subtraction, multiplication and division.

In the early Infants' school stages, children will have been partitioning sets under various relationships, such as "belongs to", "born in the month of". The concept of a set develops and the idea of "threeness" as a class of equivalent sets is discovered. From the cardinality of sets, the ordering of cardinal numbers (now known as the set of natural numbers) is undertaken, inequalities being introduced when the pupil discovers (usually by matching) that $6 > 5$ (six is greater than 5) also $5 < 6$ (five is less than 6). Relationships such as "is taller than", "is greater than", "is heavier than", "is higher than" will arise from practical work involving the environment. The time arrives when the pupils partition a set of a definite cardinality, say, 6, and from this work, the building of basic number facts begins. To assist in the discovery of these basic number facts, not only is environmental equipment such as pebbles, ribbon and string used, but commercial structural equipment (Stern, Cuisenaire, Colour Factor, Avon, etc.) may be introduced by teachers who have made a purposeful study of the equipment and know, in detail, the purpose behind its presentation.

As the operations to be discovered have *counting* as their basis, it is essential that opportunity for experiences in counting should be very carefully arranged.

In the day-to-day classroom situations there are many opportunities for real counting experience. One of these opportunities may arise at the beginning of a period when teacher says,

"Five of you can go to the water tray"
"Four may play in the Wendy House"
"Only two of you can use the sand today"

A child may play freely with the trays and objects, and as two dogs are placed in a tray one day, two horses may well be placed in the same tray on the second day, because this tray now carries the symbol 2; and it is from daily changes of spoons, cotton reels, fir cones, etc., in the same "2" tray that the idea of "twoness" is developed.

Having had experience of ordering (in size) these cardinals, the children may produce class booklets, where we find on a page perhaps a drawing and a caption, perhaps a picture and a caption, e.g.

"a chair has *four* legs"
"a table has *4* legs"
"the pram has *four* wheels"

Counting experiences may be recorded in this way (use any equipment you wish if it gives help to pupils):

Counting on in twos

$$2 \rightarrow 4 \rightarrow 6 \rightarrow 8 \rightarrow 10$$

$$3 \rightarrow 5 \rightarrow 7 \rightarrow 9$$

$$1 \rightarrow 3 \rightarrow 5 \rightarrow 7 \rightarrow 9$$

Counting on in threes

1 → 4 → 7 → 10

2 → 5 → 8 → 11

3 → 6 → 9 → 12

Counting on in fives

1 → 6 → 11 → 16

5 → 10 → 15 → 20

From these experiences, patterns in number relationships will become part of a child's mathematical thinking.

Another way of recording is,

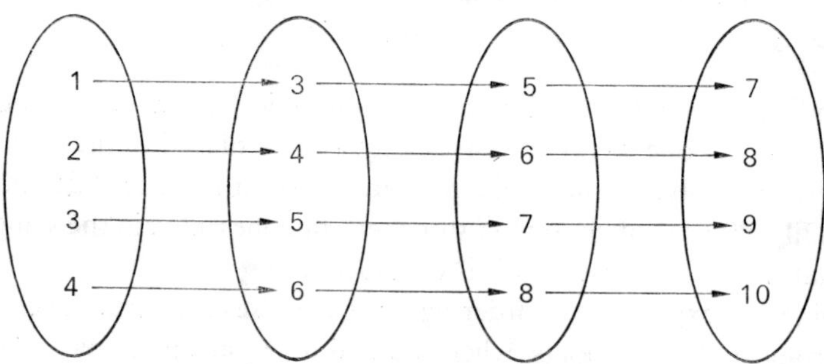

Counting on in two's

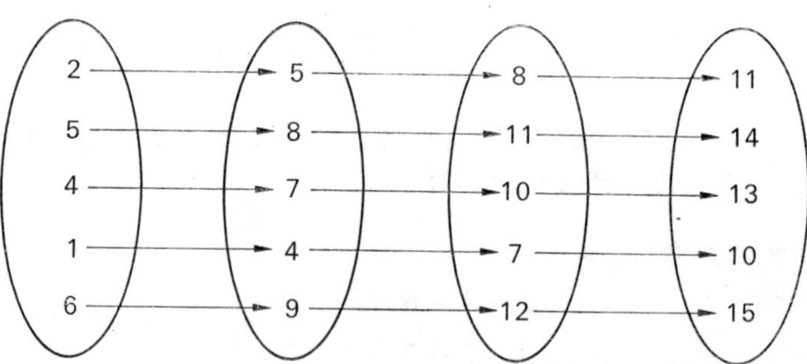

Counting on in three's

A SPECIMEN WORK CARD

Counting on in *threes*. Mark with an arrow the numeral in Set 1 which matches with the numeral in Set 2.

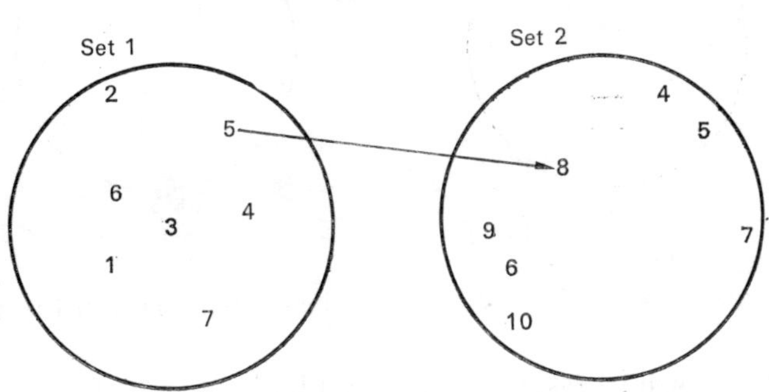

You continue the matchings. 5 has been matched with 8.

Counting down in twos

start

1 ← 3 ← 5 ← 7 ← 9

start

3 ← 5 ← 7 ← 9 ← 11 ← 13

The Story of Number

Addition facts can be introduced at this stage by using the idea of number families. We will consider the number family, FIVE.

(a) Every child concerned with this experience will have plenty of materials, such as discs, toy cats, dogs, pencils, animals he can place on a flannel board, or on a magnetic board, also a number line. The child will be asked to take 5 squares or 5 circles or 5 rectangles (use these words) or any 5 objects from his equipment and partition the set into two sets, one of them having two members. (He will have partitioned sets before, perhaps objects into two sets under the relationship "will sink when placed in water, will float when placed in water".) From discussion, he will have, say,

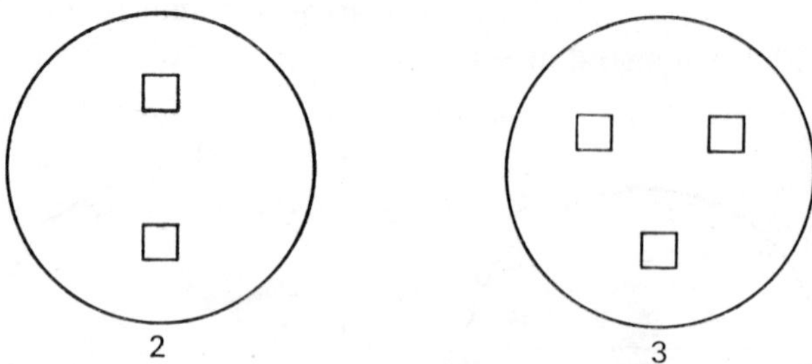

(b) He may repeat this experience on the flannel board or the magnetic board.

(c) Now he will be asked to show the addition fact by forming one set from the two sets. He will describe what he has done and record (perhaps with teacher's help).

The representation may look like this:

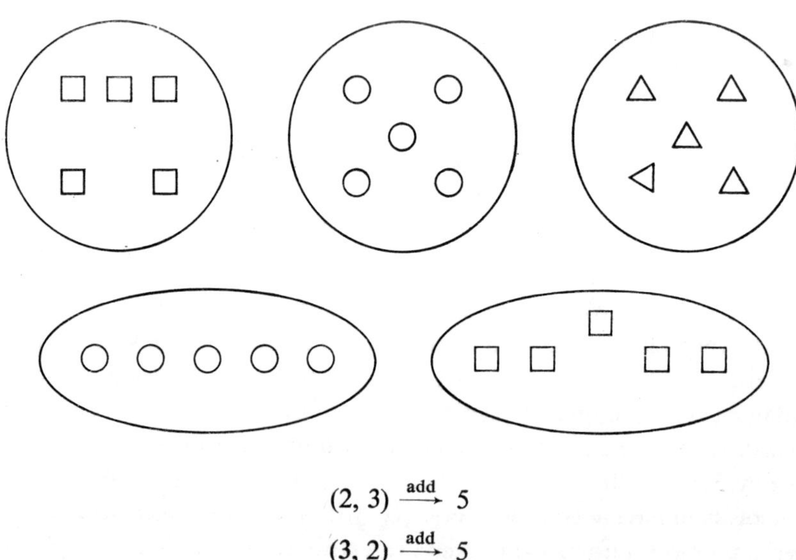

$$(2, 3) \xrightarrow{\text{add}} 5$$

$$(3, 2) \xrightarrow{\text{add}} 5$$

(d) Following discussion with the teacher, the child can be encouraged to use either the class number line or his private one, like this:

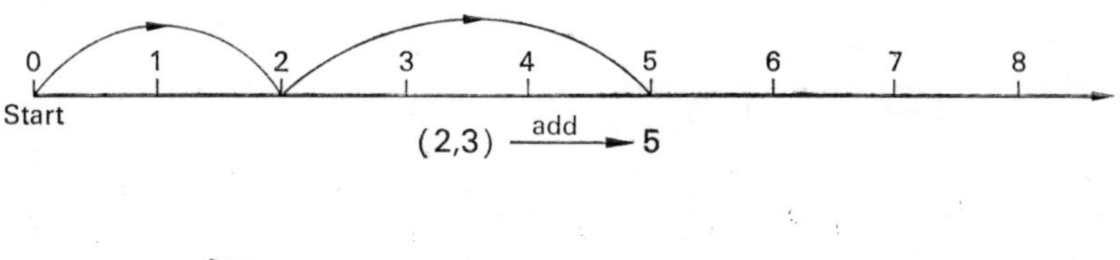

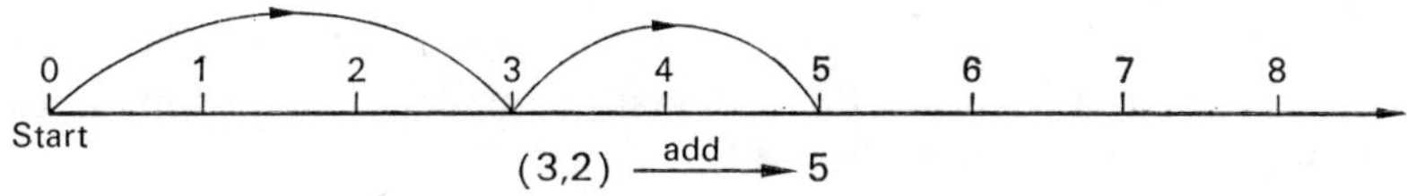

Maybe, some will record, $\begin{array}{r} 2 \\ +\,3 \\ \hline 5 \end{array}$, $2+3 \rightarrow 5$.

(e) Open sentences can be introduced.

$$(\square, 3) \xrightarrow{\text{add}} 5$$

$$(3, \square) \xrightarrow{\text{add}} 5$$

$$(2, \square) \xrightarrow{\text{add}} 5$$

$$(2, 3) \xrightarrow{\text{add}} \square$$

The idea of developing number facts by using number families has been illustrated. Only the number facts

$$(2, 3) \xrightarrow{\text{add}} 5 \quad \text{and} \quad (3, 2) \xrightarrow{\text{add}} 5$$

have been used in the illustration.

Now the children are invited to find as many addition facts, as possible, using the number family, FIVE.

Charts on the walls and the pupils' private books will contain a mass of information given by drawing pictures, captions, stories, recordings in numerals.

$$(2, 3) \xrightarrow{\text{add}} 5 \qquad 2+3 \rightarrow 5$$

$$(3, 2) \xrightarrow{\text{add}} 5 \qquad 3+2 \rightarrow 5$$

$$(1, 4) \xrightarrow{\text{add}} 5 \qquad 1+4 \rightarrow 5$$

$$(4, 1) \xrightarrow{\text{add}} 5 \qquad 4+1 \rightarrow 5$$

It is pointed out that arrows have been used instead of the symbol "=". If you decide to use this "difficult-to-understand" symbol, then the longhand explanation should be,

$$2+3 = 5$$

Say that "=" is "another way of recording" or "another name for...". *Do not use "is the same as"*, for 2+3 is NOT the same as 5. Actually (2+3), (4+1), (1+4), (3+2) are all *other ways* of writing FIVE.

From *discussion* the child may be led to generalize about the family of 5.

(a) The sums of the different number pairs can all be written as 5.
(b) There are four number pairs (in the set of natural numbers) which have a sum of 5.
(c) No members of the number pairs are of the same value. (If we were studying the family of FOUR, we should have a number pair of the same value, $(2, 2) \xrightarrow{\text{add}} 4$.)
(d) The order of writing the pairs does not matter. Addition is commutative, (2+3) = (3+2) = 5.

After the initial class discussion and experience it may be found exciting if the children, working in pairs, discover all they can about other number families, 6, 9, 10, 12, ...

The idea of "take away" may be combined with the addition facts. It should be noted that the term "take away" has been used, and not subtraction. Subtraction in mathematics will be explained later.

"Take away" can be explained physically with all the materials used for addition. "Take away" involves matching a set of objects with the ordered sequence of natural numbers.

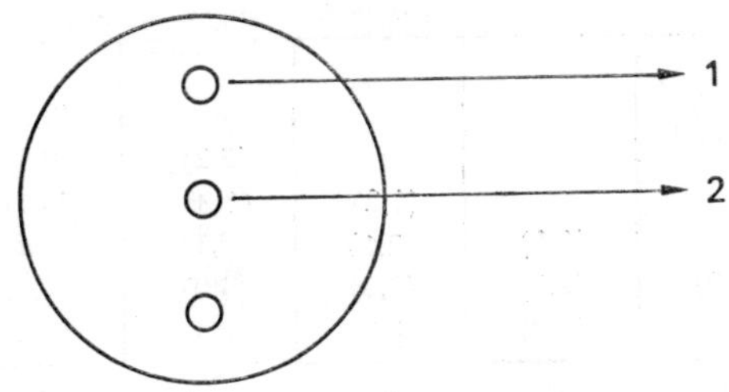

The diagram illustrates $3-2 = 1$. The number line can be used as well.

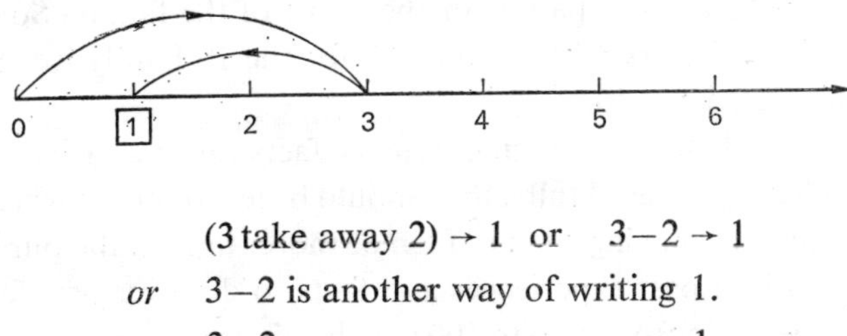

(3 take away 2) → 1 or $3-2 \rightarrow 1$

or $3-2$ is another way of writing 1.

$3-2 = 1$

or $3-2$ is another name for 1.

$3-2 = 1$

A class chart of addition facts may be very helpful.

Addition (Natural numbers)

				(3,2)	
			(2,2)	(2,3)	
		(2,1)	(3,1)	(4,1)	
	(1,1)	(1,2)	(1,3)	(1,4)	
1	2	3	4	5	

We have used the set of natural numbers up to the present. If we include zero or 0 in our set, we have the *set of whole numbers*. Now our addition chart will look like this:

Addition (Whole numbers)

				(3,2)
			(2,2)	(2,3)
		(1,2)	(1,3)	(4,1)
	(1,1)	(2,1)	(3,1)	(1,4)
(1,0)	(2,0)	(3,0)	(4,0)	(5,0)
(0,1)	(0,2)	(0,3)	(0,4)	(0,5)
1	2	3	4	5

It should be observed that if we use the set of whole numbers each number family has one *more* pair than the name of the family. So for the 4 family we have 5 pairs whose sum is 4, for the 10 family we shall have 11 pairs whose sum is 10.

If the materials for discovering number facts up to and including the family of 9 have been used fully, they should be less required when dealing with addition facts having a sum of ten or more. In fact, the pupil should be able to call on past experiences and facts to discover new facts. Perhaps a number strip from zero to 100 may be his greatest aid.

Suppose he knows and can record $(4, 5) \xrightarrow{\text{add}} 9$ or $(5, 4) \xrightarrow{\text{add}} 9$ or $4+5 = 9$. This fact should assist him in discovering $5+5 = 10$ (or any of the other ways of recording). He will say "*10 ones or 1 ten and 0 ones*".

Using his number line, he can record,

$$5+5 = 10$$

$$15+5 = 20$$

$$25+5 = 30$$

$$\cdots\cdots\cdots$$

Again, if $5+5 = 10$, further discovery can be made

$$5+6 = 11, \quad 6+5 = 11$$

(from the number line) 15+6 = 21 16+5 = 21

25+6 = 31 26+5 = 31

35+6 = 41 36+5 = 41

....

He can also discover 15+6 = 6+15 = 21 (21 ones, or 2 tens and 1 one)

25+6 = 6+25 = 31 (31 ones, or 3 tens and 1 one)

Further practical work can involve making bundles of sticks containing ten sticks. With the bundles and single sticks he arranges

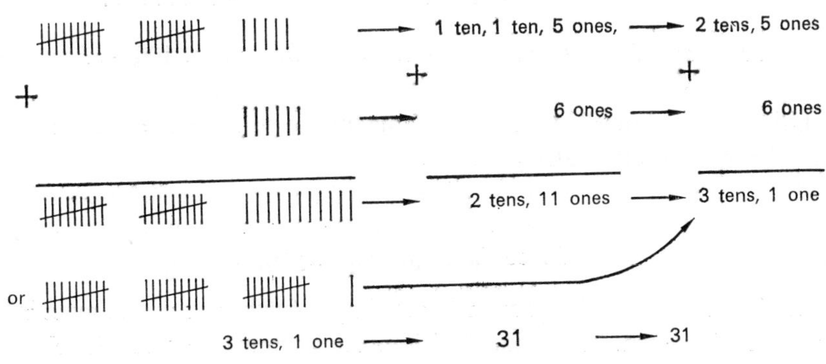

Numbers Recorded in Expanded Form

Ways of Writing 31

Children should practise different ways of writing 31. Here is an example.

31 = 30+1 = 20+11 = 26+5 = 5+26 ...

A daily 5 minutes' exercise is to ask the child to record as many ways as possible of writing a certain number. Here is an illustration.

How many different ways of writing 53 (using addition only) can you record?

e.g. $53 = 50+3 = 40+13 = 30+23 = 20+33 = 10+43$

$53 = 49+4 = 39+14 = 29+24 = 19+34 = 9+44$

$53 = 48+5 = 38+15$ ....

How many different ways of writing 23 can you record, using "take away" only?

e.g. $23 = 24-1 = 25-2 = 26-3 = 27-4 = 28-5$ ....

$23 = 30-7 = 40-17 = 50-27 = 60-37$ ...... $100-77$

Using the "bundles" idea and the number strip will give the child many experiences leading to PLACE VALUE.

Place Value (a summary)

Earlier, it was stated that counting is vital to further work and must be presented in depth. The same vital importance must be given to place value.

Place value is the dependence of the significance of a digit upon its position in a row of neighbouring digits the only variables concerned are the digits themselves and their relative positions. Materials which assist the pupil in discovering this concept include

(1) Bundles of straws, sticks, pipe cleaners ....

(2) The abacus (many types).

(3) Dienes' equipment.

A very valuable abacus is the semicircular abacus which has eighteen beads on the tens and ones wires.

Abacus Work

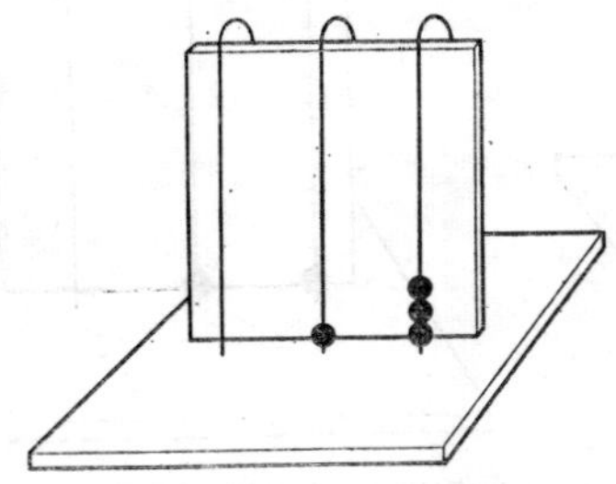

13 recorded on the abacus

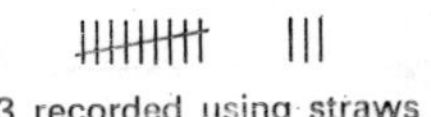

13 recorded using straws

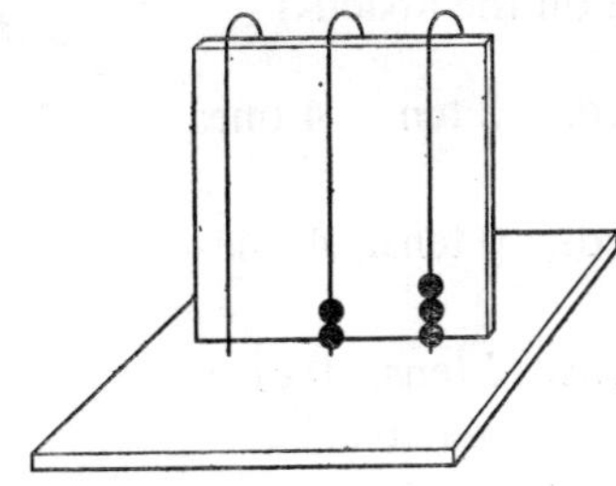

23 recorded on the abacus

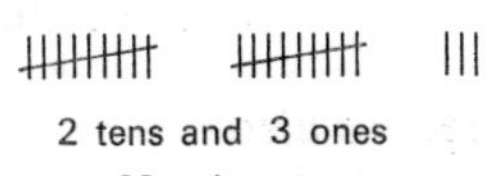

2 tens and 3 ones
23 using straws

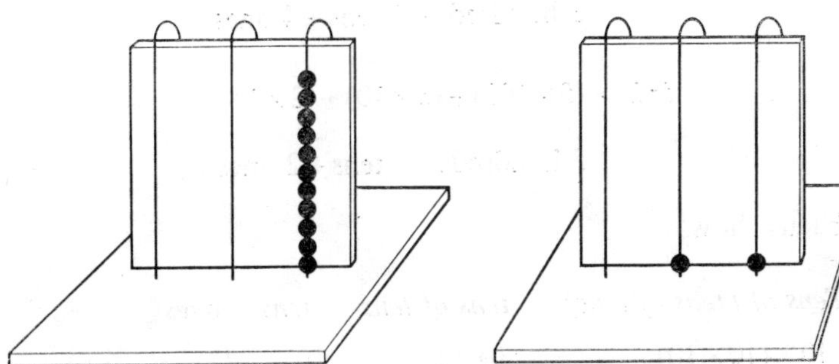

11 ones on the abacus regrouped to 1 ten 1 one

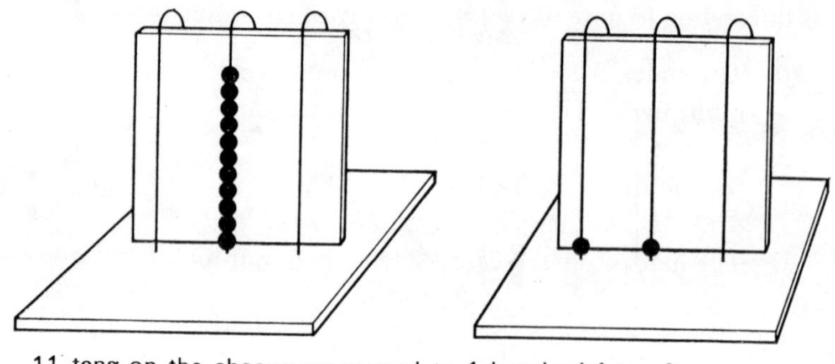

11 tens on the abacus regrouped to 1 hundred 1 ten 0 ones (110)

We can read off (after illustrating on the abacus)

324 → 3 hundreds, 2 tens, 4 ones

304 → 3 hundreds, 0 tens, 4 ones

320 → 3 hundreds, 2 tens, 0 ones

We can record also

$324 \rightarrow (3\times 100)+(2\times 10)+(4\times 1)$

3 hundreds + 2 tens + 4 ones

$562 \rightarrow (5\times 100)+(6\times 10)+(2\times 1)$

5 hundreds + 6 tens + 2 ones

Our abacus shows

Tens of (tens of tens)	*tens of tens*	*tens*	*ones*
$10\times(10\times 10)$	10×10	10	1
10^3	10^2	10^1	ones (by pattern 10^0)
1000	100	10	1

It is interesting to note the very short way of recording these values.

e.g. 10^3 The index 3 tells us how many times to record 10 (ten) before multiplying. Here we record 10 three times:

10, 10, 10

then multiply $10\times10\times10 = 1000$

So 10^3 is another way of writing 1000.

10^2 The index 2 says "record 2 tens then multiply":

10, 10

10×10

100

So 10^2 is another way of writing 100.

Place numbers on an abacus, then show any ways you can of writing the numbers you have chosen.

Example. Place 334 on an abacus.

3 ways of writing 334

$300+30+4$. $(3\times100)+(3\times10)+(4\times1)$

$(3\times10^2)+(3\times10^1)+4$

It may be a pupil, calling on past experiences, will *also* record such statements as

$$334 = 340-6 = 300+20+14$$

The Addition Algorithm

Now study *the stages* in this addition example.

$$\begin{array}{r}35\\+27\\\hline\end{array} \rightarrow \underset{\text{(a)}}{\begin{array}{r}30+5\\+(20+7)\\\hline 50+12\end{array}} \rightarrow \underset{\text{(b)}}{\begin{array}{r}35\\+27\\\hline 12\\50\\\hline 62\end{array}} \rightarrow \underset{\text{(c)}}{\begin{array}{r}\boxed{1}\\35\\+27\\\hline 62\end{array}} \rightarrow \underset{\text{(d)}}{\begin{array}{r}35\\+27\\\hline 62\end{array}}$$

(In (a)–(b), arrows lead from 12 and from 50 of "50+12" to the 12 and 50 in (b).)

(a) The numbers are written in expanded form and the addition recorded.

(b) The numbers are not expanded but the "ones" result then the "tens" result from (a) are recorded separately. (The idea of the "appropriate columns" (of place value), i.e. tens column, ones column, is developed in this way.)

(c) □ is filled with the number of tens which has been formed by exchanging the "ones" for bundles of ten, and transferring the result to the appropriate "tens" column.

(d) The entire operation is carried out mentally without use of any "crutches".

Further examples:

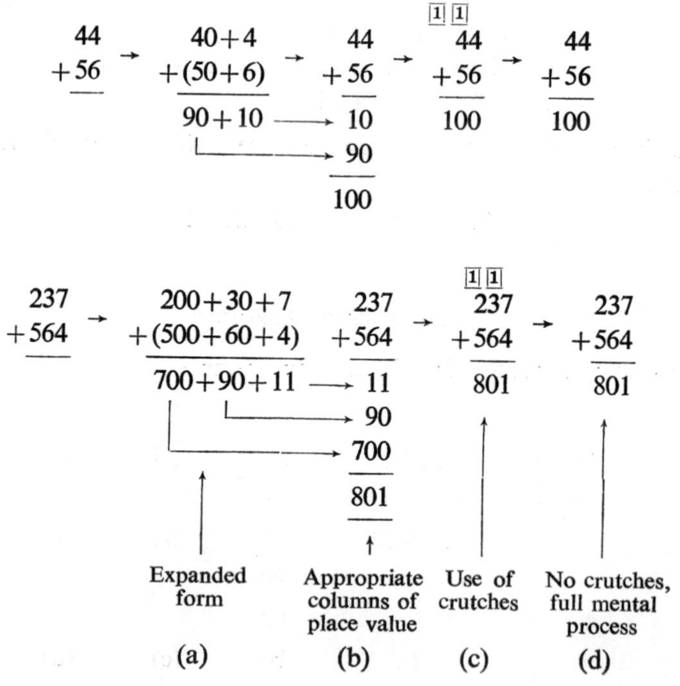

```
 44      40+4        44    [1][1]    44
+56  → +(50+6)  →  +56  →   44   → +56
       -------     ---     +56      ---
        90+10 ──→   10     ---      100
         └──────→   90     100
                   ---
                   100
```

```
 237      200+30+7        237    [1][1]      237
+564  → +(500+60+4)      +564  →   237   →  +564
        -----------      ----     +564      ----
        700+90+11 ──→     11      ----       801
         |   └──────→     90       801        ↑
         └──────────→    700        ↑         |
             ↑           ----       |         |
             |            801       |         |
             |             ↑        |         |
         Expanded    Appropriate  Use of   No crutches,
           form      columns of   crutches  full mental
                     place value             process
            (a)          (b)        (c)        (d)
```

It may be many children will omit (c). "Crutches" can be unhelpful! They can inculcate lazy thinking.

If the operation of addition is understood and practical work has been given involving exchange of measures, then the addition of number and measures can be developed simultaneously.

29
+15
→
20+9
+(10+5)
30+14 → 14
└──→ 30
44
29
+15
14
30
44
→
29
+15
44

m cm
2 79
+1 35
3 114 → 1 14
└──→ 3 0
4 14
→
m cm
2 79
+1 35
1 14
3 0
4 14
→
m cm
1
2 79
+1 35
4 14
→
m cm
2 79
+1 35
4 14

£ new pennies £
2 80 → 2.80
+1 30 → 1.30
3 110 → 1.10
└──→ 3.
£ 4.10

Study these examples of children's computation arising from a classroom situation. 19 boys and 14 girls from Class 3A are to visit a Road

Safety lecture at 2.30 p.m. How many children from 3A will leave school early?

(a)
$$\begin{array}{r} 19 \\ +14 \\ \hline 13 \\ 20 \\ \hline 33 \\ \hline \end{array}$$

(b)
$$\begin{array}{rl} 19 & \\ +14 & \\ \hline 20 & \\ 13 & \\ \hline 33 & \text{children} \\ \hline \end{array}$$

(c)
$$\begin{array}{r} 19 \\ +14 \end{array} \rightarrow \begin{array}{r} 20 \\ +14 \\ \hline 34 \\ 33 \end{array}$$

$$\begin{array}{c} (+1) \\ (-1) \end{array} \left[\begin{array}{c} (+1) \text{ and } (-1) \\ \text{results in} \\ \bigcirc \end{array} \right]$$

(d)
$$\begin{array}{r} 14 \\ +19 \\ \hline 13 \\ 20 \\ \hline 33 \\ \hline \end{array}$$

(e)
$$\begin{array}{r} 14 \\ +20 \\ \hline 34 \\ -\ 1 \\ \hline 33 \\ \hline \end{array}$$

(f)
$$\begin{array}{r} 24 \\ +\ 9 \\ \hline 33 \\ \hline \end{array}$$

(g)
$$\begin{array}{r} 29 \\ +\ 4 \\ \hline 33 \\ \hline \end{array}$$

(h) 33

Each child explained the method used.
Each child was given a word of praise!

CHAPTER 7

SUBTRACTION (GENERAL THOUGHTS)

PROBABLY the most harmful phrase used in the classroom is "Three from two, *I can't*". Although it sounds reasonable at the time and "gets it over", later in his career the child will find "Three from two, *I can*", and a barrier has been set up. He finds a meaning to -1 which is as "real" a number as $+1$. The situation is this:

"Using the set of natural numbers, I cannot find a solution to 'Three from two', but if I was considering the set of integers, I could find a solution." Now we do not say this to the child. It is preferred to use the language illustrated later in this chapter.

Should we teach subtraction in the primary school just because $3-5$ seems to put up a barrier?

We should certainly teach the idea of difference which arises from comparing a set of objects with a set of objects. We should teach "take away" which is a physical operation during which we are matching a set of objects with the ordered sequence of natural numbers.

We may express the idea of subtraction in terms of addition, e.g.

$$5-3=\square \Rightarrow 3+\square=5.$$

From the mathematical aspect, what is subtraction?

We answer this question by considering a miniature arithmetical system which contains all the features we need. We will consider the dial on an electric cooker, or heater.

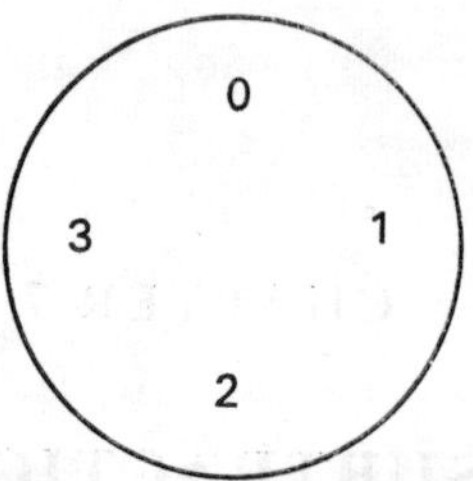

Here the set of numbers under consideration is {0, 1, 2, 3}.
On the heater in my room these numerals are replaced by

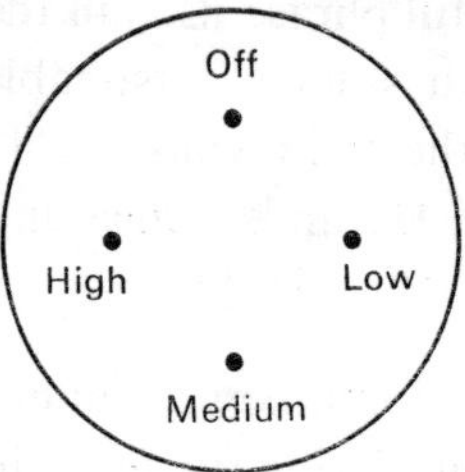

The set {0, 1, 2, 3} could be the set of remainders when we divide any number by 4. Here the system is known as arithmetic modulo 4.

In this system every number has an "additive inverse". This means that whatever number we start with we can find a number which, when added to the first one, gives 0.

The additive inverse of 3 is 1 because $3+1 = 0$.

Here is the complete list for the set {0, 1, 2, 3}, i.e. mod. 4.

Number	*Additive inverse*
0	0
1	3
2	2
3	1

$a-b$, i.e. "Subtraction" in this system means "Find the additive inverse of b and add it to a".

For example, $2-3$ (mod. 4) means "Find the additive inverse of 3 and add it to 2 (using mod. 4)".

The additive inverse of 3 (mod. 4) is 1.

$$2+1 = 3 \text{ (mod. 4)}$$

$$\text{so} \quad 2-3 \text{ (mod. 4)} = 3$$

Test by moving back three stages the pointer on the heater from Medium (2). The point will arrive at High (3).

So subtraction is defined as "addition of the additive inverse".

If we are in the set of natural numbers we find we have no additive inverse to the natural number. It was because of this that man invented the set of integers. In this system of integers subtraction is always possible for each positive integer has an additive inverse. Therefore in the set of naturals you cannot subtract three from two or two from three. You can physically remove two from three or compare a set of three objects with a set of two objects.

When working in the set of integers you can record

$$\begin{array}{r} 32 \\ -19 \\ \hline 20+-7 \\ 13 \end{array}$$

We use the set of integers so that $a-b$ always has a meaning and $x+b = a$ has a solution.

Summary

$$5-4 \text{ (natural numbers)}$$

You cannot subtract. The set of naturals does not contain an additive inverse of 4.

$$+5-+4 \text{ (integers)}$$

You can subtract. This statement reads: "Find the additive inverse of $+4$ and add it to $+5$."

The additive inverse of $+4$ is -4.

$$+5 + -4 = +1.$$

These ideas are for the student to think about.

We will move into the classroom with our thoughts on the subtraction algorithm.

The Subtraction Algorithm

We are concerned with the set of natural numbers.

$$\{1, 2, 3, 4, 5 \ldots\}$$

We can add two natural numbers and the result will be a natural number. The set of natural numbers is closed under addition. We can "take away" two from five $(5-2)$ and the result 3 is a natural number. But $2-5$ cannot give a result in the set of natural numbers. In order to find a result to $2-5$, man had to invent another system, the set of integers. We shall look at this set later. *At present we are only considering the set of natural numbers*, and in this set we cannot carry out true subtraction (again, subtraction will be defined later when we consider integers).

We will consider the "subtraction" operation, however, in terms of "difference" and "take away".

Difference involves COMPARING two sets by matching:

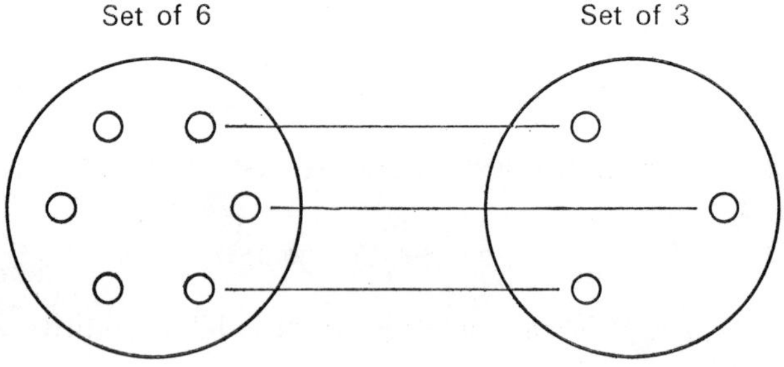

We compare a set of six objects with a set of three objects. The lines show the matching. We find we have three objects *unmatched*. The cardinal number of this *unmatched* subset is known as the *difference*.

We record $6-3 = 3.$

> *Matching a set of objects with a set of objects* leads us to a cardinal number of the subset which is unmatched. This cardinal number is known as the *difference*.

The "take away" idea involves a physical removal. We have a set of six conkers and we *physically remove* three of them. We are still matching, but this time we are *matching* the conkers we remove with the ordered sequence of the *set of counting numbers*. We may count silently as we "take away".

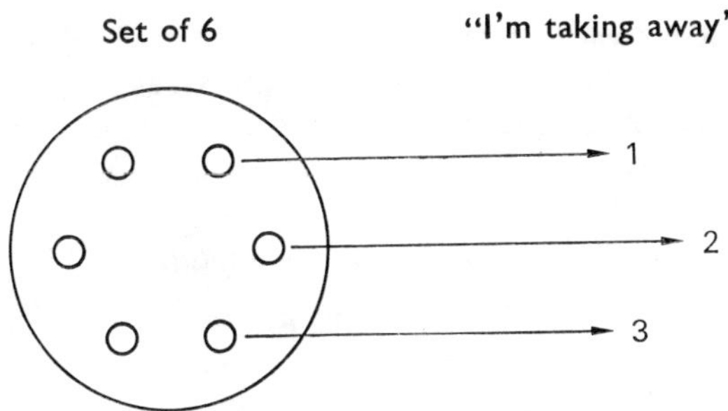

The cardinal number of the subset unmatched (not physically taken away) is the number *left*. Again, we can record

$$6-3 = 3$$

> Matching a set with the ordered sequence of counting numbers (we may say them or think them) leads us to the cardinal number of a subset not removed. This cardinal number tells us how many are left.

Special Note

We know also from the examples given that $6 > 3$.
(6 is greater than 3).

We will look at the idea of expressing the "subtraction" in terms of addition.

$$6-2$$

This statement asks a question, $2+\square \overset{?}{=} 6$

(2 and some number is another way of writing 6) or
(2 and some number is another name for 6).
The truth set is 4—usually written $\{4\}$.

$5-3$ can be written $3+\square = 5$. This is an open sentence. The truth set is $\{2\}$.

Q. Write in addition form $8-4$, $12-6$, $17-13$, $89-57$, $126-63$.

A. $4+\square = 8$; $6+\square = 12$; $13+\square = 17$; $57+\square = 89$; $63+\square = 126$.

Subtraction is not commutative

$$6-3 \neq 3-6.$$

Subtraction is not associative

$$12-(6-2) \neq (12-6)-2.$$

This statement is true

$$(a-0) = a; \quad 7-0 = 7.$$

The following are some examples of development for you to study.

Find the difference between 8 and 5

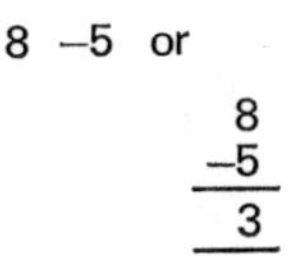

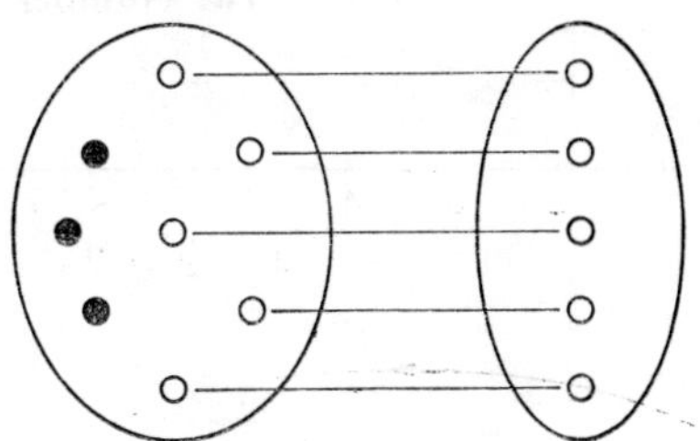

Take away 5 from 8

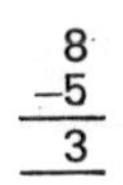

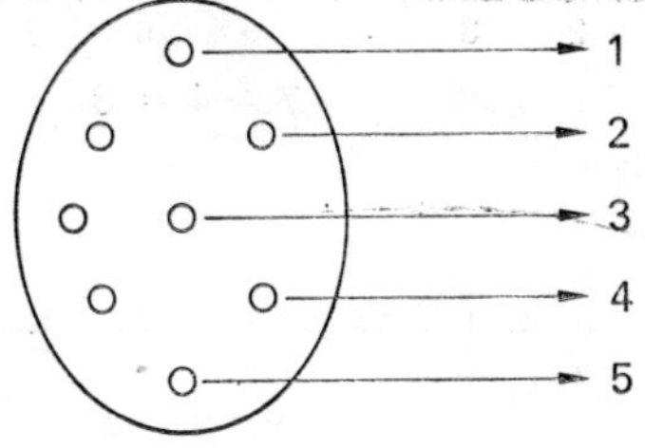

RELATIONSHIP BETWEEN ADDITION AND SUBTRACTION

$$4+3 = 7 \text{ and } 7-3 = 4 \quad \text{also} \quad 7-4 = 3.$$

Remember $7-3 = 4$ *because* $4+3 = 7$.

Study Carefully

We begin with a number, say 7. We add a number, say 2, then we subtract this same number 2. We return to the number we had at the beginning.

Recording $\qquad (7+2)-2 = 7$

$$(a+b)-b = a.$$

This idea is very important later on.

Relationship between addition and subtraction.

$$7-3 \text{ states } 3+\square = 7$$

$$12-8 \text{ states } 8+\square = 12.$$

The Number Line

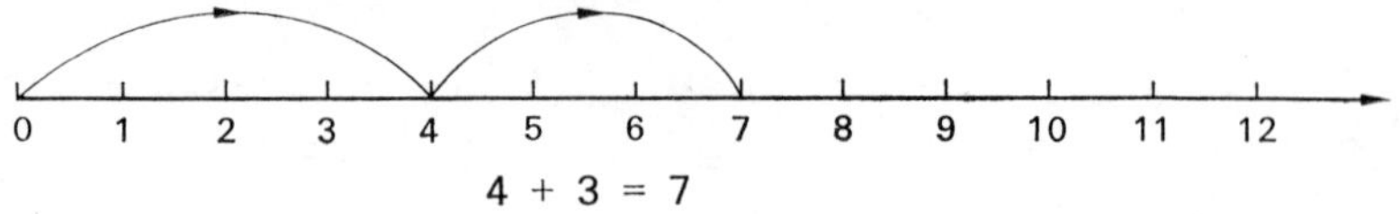

$4 + 3 = 7$

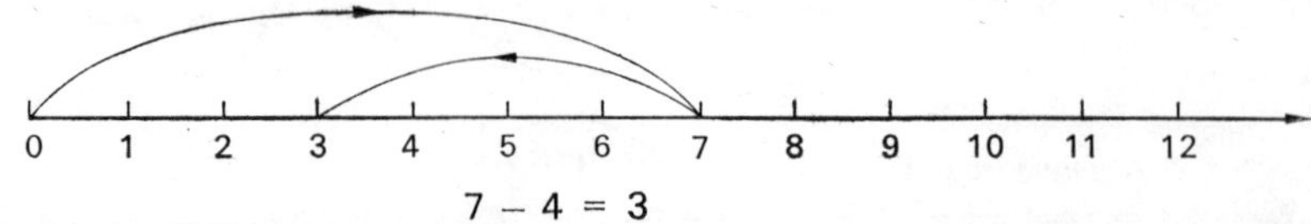

$7 - 4 = 3$

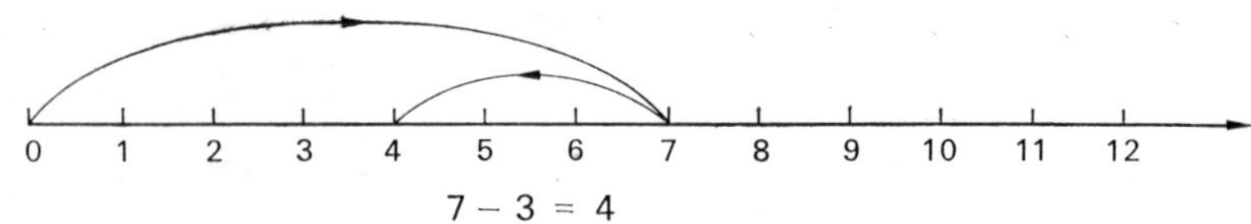

$7 - 3 = 4$

NOTE

$(7-3)-2$	$12-(5-1)$
$4-2$	$12-4$
2	8

Using Bundles or the Abacus

From a situation we have $32-13$.

$$\begin{array}{r} 32 \\ -13 \\ \hline \end{array}$$

The 13 we remove is contained in the 32.
Therefore the recorded 13 tells us only what to remove from 32.
It is a recording which is not part of the physical process.

$$\begin{array}{r} 32 \\ -13 \\ \hline \end{array} \rightarrow \underset{(a)}{\begin{array}{r} 30+2 \\ -(10+3) \\ \hline \end{array}} \rightarrow \underset{(b)}{\begin{array}{r} 20+12 \\ -(10+3) \\ \hline 10+9 \\ \hline \end{array}} \rightarrow \underset{(c)}{\begin{array}{r} \boxed{2}\,\boxed{12} \\ 32 \\ -13 \\ \hline 19 \\ \hline \end{array}} \rightarrow \underset{(d)}{\begin{array}{r} 32 \\ -13 \\ \hline 19 \\ \hline \end{array}}$$

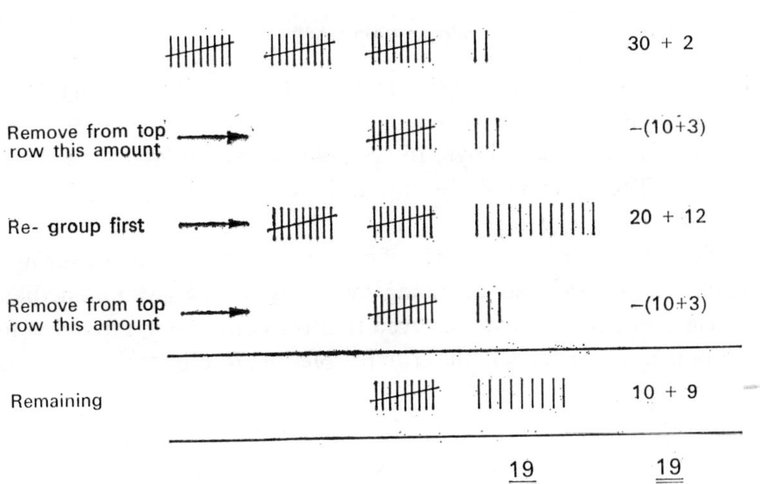

(a) 30+2 is another name for 32.

10+3 is another name for 13.

(b) As the names 32 and 13 in (a) are not helpful in finding a result, we use more convenient names.
20+12 is a more convenient way (in this situation) of naming 32.
We carry out the subtraction.

(c) We use "crutches". Some children may disregard them. So much the better if they do.

[2] → 20 [12] → necessary to carry out the operation.

(d) Immediate mental regrouping. No "crutches".

We are concerned with removing 13 from the set of 32. Really we partition 32 objects into 2 subsets, 1 subset having 13 elements. The number of members of the other subset is our target of discovery.

Points to Note

1. Always start with a *situation* to show the need for carrying out the operation, e.g.

    Out of a class of 33 boys, 16 are going to Wembley to see the Cup Final. The remainder say they will view on television. How many boys will be viewing?

2. If the classes have had plenty of practical experience in measuring and weighing, their examples involving measures can be given immediately.

3. The student will have observed that the convenient expanded form corresponds to the entry in the crutches section. Really there is no need to use crutches.

CHAPTER 8

MULTIPLICATION

Sets: The Cartesian Product of Two Sets*

We are going to consider multiplication, using the set of natural numbers, and we begin by looking at a special operation on sets.

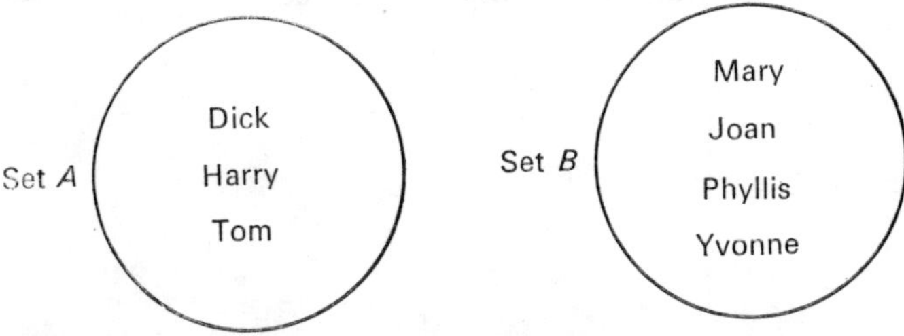

We have a set of boys {Dick, Harry, Tom} and set of girls {Mary, Joan, Phyllis, Yvonne} at a Youth Club dance and *each* boy of Set A is going to dance with *every* girl in Set B. How does it work out?

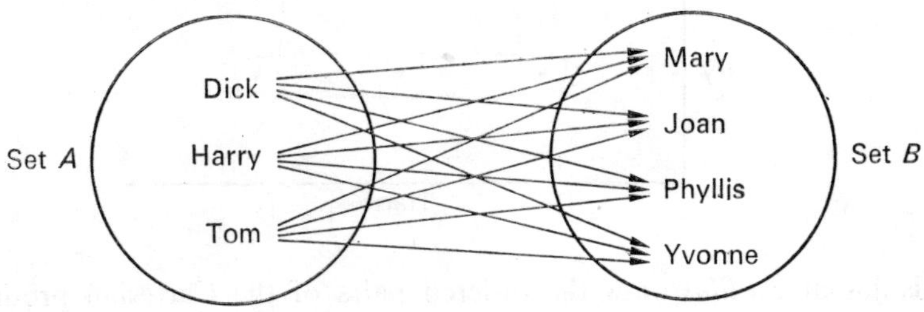

* See Chapter 3.

We have carried out a sample matching. The set of possible pairs will be:

{(Dick, Mary), (Dick, Joan), (Dick, Phyllis), (Dick, Yvonne), (Harry, Mary), (Harry, Joan), (Harry, Phyllis), (Harry, Yvonne), (Tom, Mary), (Tom, Joan), (Tom, Phyllis), (Tom, Yvonne)}

The sets of pairs given illustrate the idea known as the *Cartesian product* of two sets. We have paired *each* member of the first set A with every member of the *second* set B. This set of ordered pairs (ordered because the boys' names from Set A are always first) gives us the Cartesian product of the two sets, A and B (written $A \times B$, i.e. "A cross B").

It will be observed, that the cardinal number of Set A is 3, of Set B, 4, and of the set ordered pairs, 12. There are 3 members in Set A and for *each* member in Set A, there are 4 members in Set B with which it can be paired. Further, there are 12 pairs in $A \times B$ (A cross B).

We can now illustrate these pairs on a lattice.

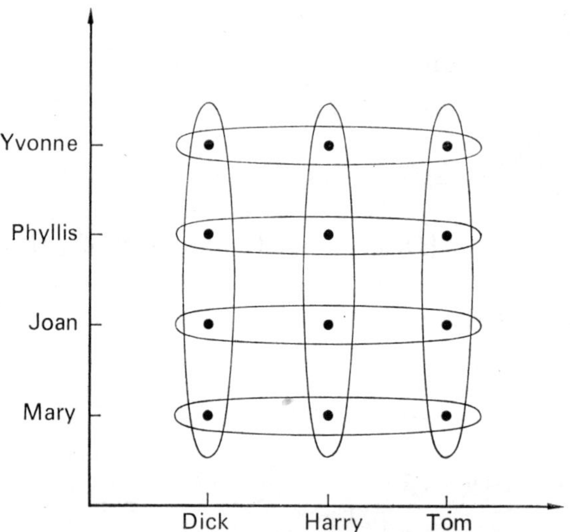

This dot array *illustrates* the ordered pairs of the Cartesian product, ($A \times B$). If we study it closely, we shall observe that it contains:

	In terms of addition
4 sets of 3	$3+3+3+3$
3 sets of 4	$4+4+4$

The cardinal number of the product set (12) is the *product of the cardinal numbers of the sets.*

Really, we have reduced our pairs to COUNTING. Looking at the array of points on our lattice, we could count them in ones, twos, threes, fours, sixes and twelves:

12×1

6×2

4×3

2×6

1×12

We can observe also that the set of the factors of 12 is {1, 2, 3, 4, 6, 12}.

Let us study another example.

There are 2 roads from Abdon to Bedon and 3 roads from Bedon to Cedon. In how many possible ways can I get from Abdon to Cedon?

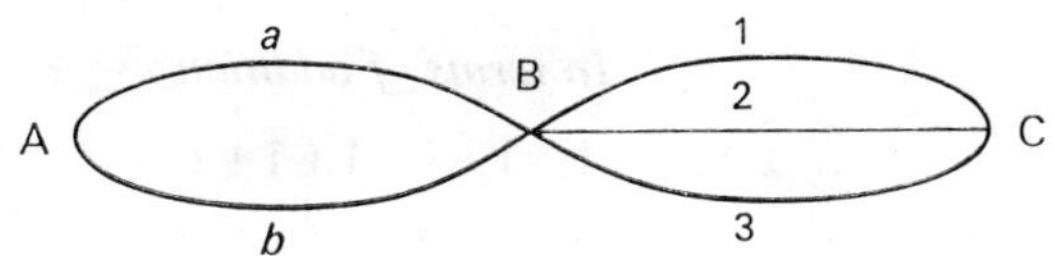

From A to B we have 2 roads, from B to C, 3 roads.

The routes, written in ordered pairs are

$(a, 1), \quad (a, 2), \quad (a, 3)$

$(b, 1), \quad (b, 2), \quad (b, 3)$

If the roads from A to B belong to Set A and from B to C to Set B, then the cardinal numbers of the Cartesian product ($A\times B$) will be 6. Each member of Set A has been matched with *every* member of Set B. There are 2 members in Set A, 3 members in Set B, and 6 pairs in $A \times B$ (A cross B). Again, the cardinal number of the product set is *the product of the cardinal numbers of the sets A and B.*

Illustrating on a lattice, we have

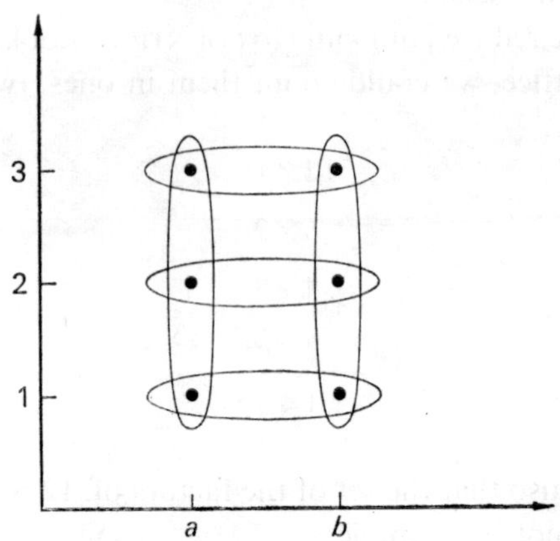

We have placed the product set on a lattice. We can count this dot array in ones, twos, threes and sixes.

	In terms of addition
6×1	$1+1+1+1+1+1$
3×2	$2+2+2$
2×3	$3+3$
1×6	6

Study these sets

$$A = \{1, 2, 3, 4\}, \qquad B = \{\ \} \quad \text{the empty set.}$$

How many ordered pairs can we form from the Cartesian product $A \times B$? We cannot form any, for we cannot match Set A with nothing.

There are 4 elements in Set A and none in Set B, so $A \times B$ produces no ordered pairs.

We can state, therefore, that $n(A)\times n(B) = n(A\times B)$

$$\text{or} \quad 4\times 0 = 0$$

Now we will consider the sets

$$A = \{1, 2\} \quad B = \{1\}$$

The Cartesian product will produce

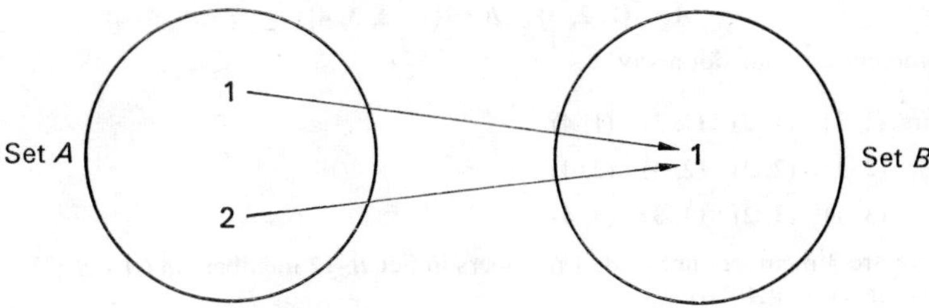

the ordered pairs (1, 1) and (2, 1).

There are 2 members in Set A and 1 member in Set B. For each member in Set A there is only 1 member in Set B with which it can be paired. There are *two* pairs in the Cartesian product $A\times B$ (A cross B).

Illustrated on a lattice and reduced to counting, we have

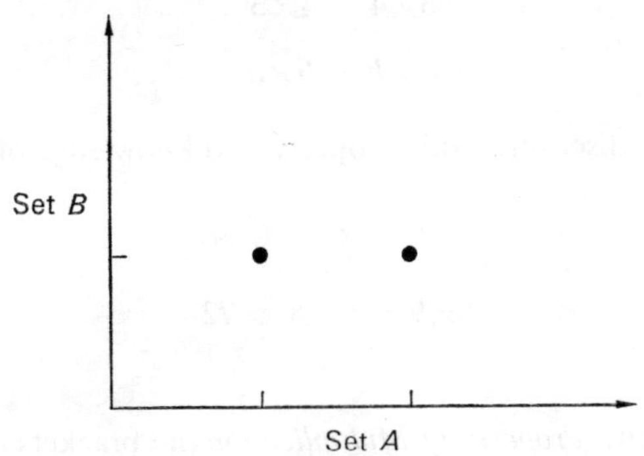

$n(A)\times n(B) = n(A\times B)$	*in terms of addition*
$2\times 1 = 2$	$1+1$

From our last two examples, we have discovered

$$n \times 0 = 0$$

$$n \times 1 = n$$

Q. Find the product set, $A \times B$, of this pair of sets and illustrate your ordered pairs on a lattice.

$$A = \{1, 2, 3\} \quad B = \{1, 2, 3, 4\}.$$

Comment on your dot array.

A. Pairs (1, 1) (1, 2) (1, 3) (1, 4)
(2, 1) (2, 2) (2, 3) (2, 4)
(3, 1) (3, 2) (3, 3) (3, 4)

There are 3 members in Set A, 4 members in Set B, 12 members in $(A \times B)$; $n(A) \times n(B) = n(A \times B)$.

Properties of Multiplication

The Commutative Property of Multiplication

$$3 \times 4 = 4 \times 3$$

$$a \times b = b \times a$$

Pupils who have discovered this property find knowledge of tables much easier, e.g.

$$7 \times 8 = 8 \times 7 = 56$$

$$8 \times 9 = 9 \times 8 = 72$$

The Associative Property of Multiplication (no brackets required)

$$3 \times (4 \times 5) = (3 \times 4) \times 5$$

$$a \times (b \times c) = (a \times b) \times c$$

The Identity Element for Multiplication

$$3\times 1 = 3$$

$$n\times 1 = n$$

We can use these properties (like we did with addition) to simplify our work.

$5\times(2\times 6)$	$(18\times 4)\times 25$
$(5\times 2)\times 6$	$18\times(4\times 25)$
10×6	18×100
$\underline{60}$	$\underline{1800}$

Use some properties of multiplication to rearrange,

$(a\times b)\times c \rightarrow b\times(c\times a)$

$(a\times b)\times c \rightarrow (b\times a)\times c$ (Commutative property)

then $(b\times a)\times c \rightarrow b\times(a\times c)$ (Associative property)

and $b\times(a\times c) \rightarrow b\times(c\times a)$ (Commutative property)

and $b\times(c\times a)$ is the arrangement of $(a\times b)\times c$ required.

Q. Use the associative property to simplify these statements.
(i) $2\times(5\times 3)$; (ii) $(7\times 12)\times 5$; (iii) $(18\times 50)\times 2$;
(iv) $(60\times 25)\times 4$; (v) $8\times(5\times 9)$; (vi) $4\times(2\times 9)$

A. (i) $(2\times 5)\times 3$; (ii) $7\times(12\times 5)$; (iii) $18\times(50\times 2)$;
(iv) $60\times(25\times 4)$; (v) $(8\times 5)\times 9$; (vi) $(4\times 2)\times 9$.

Q. *In terms of addition*

[16]	(a) $4+4+4+4$	[16] 4 sets of 4,	[16] 4 fours,	$4\times 4 =$ [16]
for you	(b) $8+8+8+8$	[32]	....	....
	(c) $9+9+9+9$	....	....	....

A. (b) 4 sets of 8, 4 eights, $4\times 8 = 32$.
(c) 4 sets of 9, 4 nines, $4\times 9 = 36$.

Build up arrays, like this (have 100 squares for your equipment). *We will have 8 squares in the base row.*

Row 1 (base row) □ □ □ □ □ □ □ □ 1x8 = 8

Row No.
2 □ □ □ □ □ □ □ □ 2x8 = 16
(base row) 1 □ □ □ □ □ □ □ □ 2 rows of 8 = 16
2 sets of 8 = 16

Turn through 90 degrees.

Row No.
8 □ □
7 □ □
6 □ □
5 □ □
4 □ □
3 □ □ 8x2 = 16
2 □ □ 8 rows of 2 = 16
(base row) 1 □ □ 8 sets of 2 = 16

So $2\times 8 = 8\times 2 = 16$ (the Commutative property applies).

Q. Pupils are able to build up and discover their multiplication facts by this array method. Try it with base rows of 7, 8 and 9.

Q. Build up arrays to illustrate:

7+7+7
4 eights
8 fours
3 nines
3×12

Q. We will use a base row of 9. Build up a rectangular array and record:

No. in base row	*No. of rows*	*Total squares*
9	1	9
9	2	18
9	3	27
.	.	.
.	.	.
.	.	.

Q. Complete this tabulation (using equipment if you wish):

No. in base row	*No. of rows*	*Total squares*
8	4	□
8	□	56
8	□	32
□	5	25
8	□	72
□	9	72
6	□	54
□	9	54

USING A NUMBER LINE

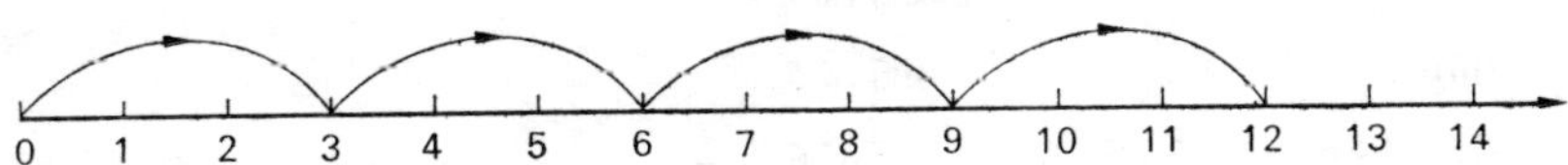

Here we illustrate 4 sets of 3. The point we reach is 12.

$$4\times 3 = 12, \quad \text{4 sets of 3} = 12$$

We could record $(4, 3) \xrightarrow{\text{multiply}} 12$, $(4, 3) \rightarrow 12$.

$$4\times 3 = 12$$

$$3+3+3+3 = 12$$

Q. Record these illustrations using the method suggested above.

(i)

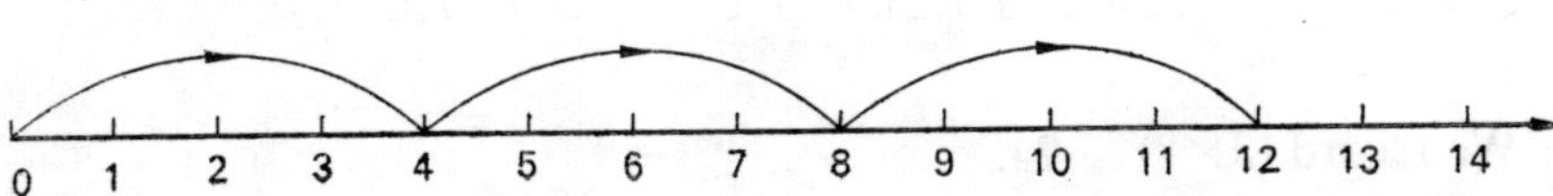

(ii)

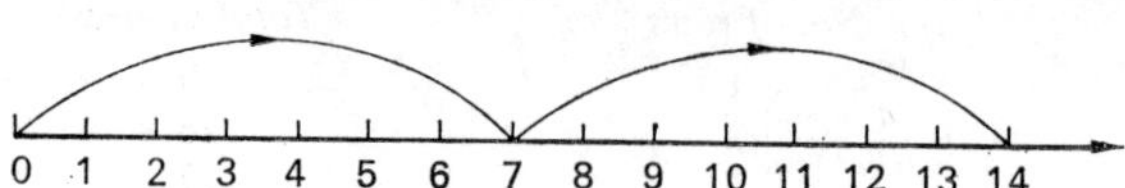

(iii)

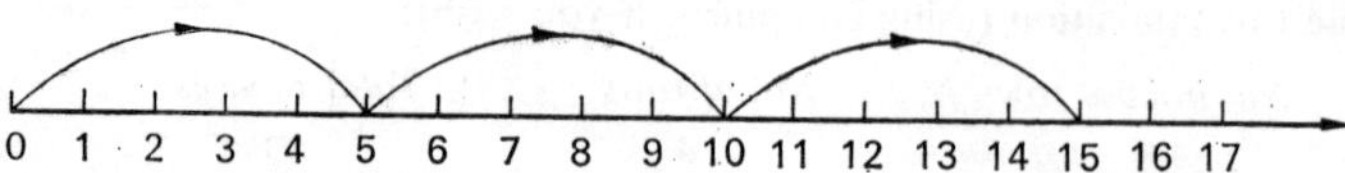

(iv)

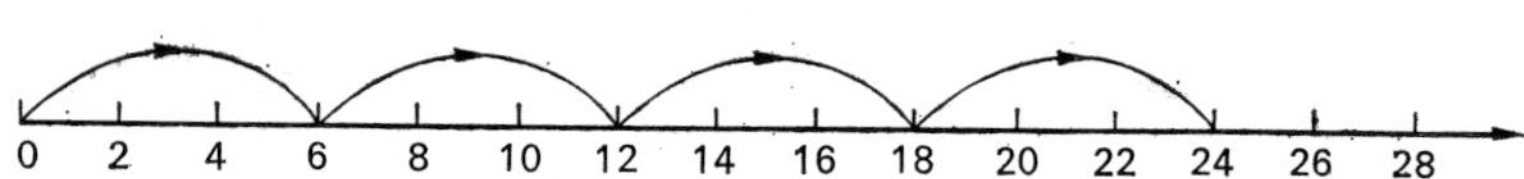

A. (i)	3×4	4+4+4	3 sets of 4
(ii)	2×7	7+7	2 sets of 7
(iii)	3×5	5+5+5	3 sets of 5
(iv)	4×6	6+6+6+6	4 sets of 6

We will look in some detail at this array

We record (3×8) = 24.

Now we will partition this set of 24.

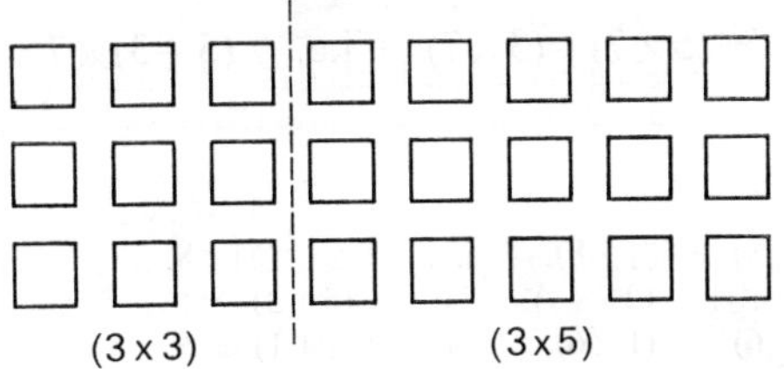

$$(3\times3)+(3\times5) = 3\times(3+5) = 3\times8$$

so 3×8 can be recorded as $3\times(3+5)$

$\rightarrow (3\times3)+(3\times5)$

$9 + 15$

$\underline{24}$

We are distributing the operation of multiplication over addition, from the left.

$$3\times8 = 8\times3 = 24$$

We could record,

8×3

$8\times(2+1)$

$(8\times2)+(8\times1)$

$16 + 8$

$\underline{24}$

or

$(4+4)\times3$

$(4\times3)+(4\times3)$

$12 + 12$

$\underline{24}$

(Distributing multiplication over addition from the right)

In the mathematical world 3×8 and 8×3 are ways of writing or naming 24. In the physical world there is a difference. In fact it could be serious!

3 lengths of wood each 8 m in length could cause anger to the "do-it-yourself" man who required

8 lengths of wood each 3 m in length.

Here are some more examples of distribution of multiplication over addition.

$$8\times 7 = (5\times 7)+(3\times 7), \quad \text{i.e.} \quad (5+3)\times 7$$

Q. Try these:

(a) $9\times 8 = (6\times 8) + (\square\times 8)$, i.e. $(\triangle+\square)\times 8$.
(b) $8\times 9 = (5\times\square) + (3\times\square)$, i.e. $(5+3)\times\square$.
(c) $7\times 6 = (\square\times 6) + (1\times 6)$, i.e. $(\square+1)\times 6$.

A. (a) (3×8), i.e. $(6+3)\times 8$
(b) $(5\times 9)+(3\times 9)$, i.e. $(5+3)\times 9$
(c) $(6\times 6)+(1\times 6)$, i.e. $(6+1)\times 6$

Study this example:

$$\begin{array}{r} 15 \\ \times 12 \\ \hline \end{array}$$

When you are carrying out this operation you may begin with (15×2) then (15×10) and add your results.
You may also begin with (15×10) then (15×2) and add your results.

Whichever beginning point you make you are distributing multiplication over addition.

$$15\times(10+2) \quad \text{or} \quad 15\times(2+10)$$

$$(15\times 10)+(15\times 2) \quad \text{or} \quad (15\times 2)+(15\times 10)$$

Again, $(6\times 10)+(3\times 10)$ can be written as $(6+3)\times 10$

$$(9\times 10)$$

$$\underline{90}$$

Q. *Short cut these statements* and check your results:

(i) $(4\times 12)+(3\times 12)$, $(7\times 8)+(2\times 8)$
(ii) $(8\times 5)+(8\times 3)$, $(9\times 5)+(9\times 3)$
(iii) $(7\times 5)+(5\times 5)$, $(6\times 8)+(2\times 8)$
(iv) $(6\times 8)+(3\times 8)$, $(10\times 11)+(1\times 11)$

A. (i) 7×12, 9×8; (ii) 8×8, 9×8;
(iii) 12×5, 8×8; (iv) 9×8, 11×11.

Complete the sentences using the symbols, = or > or < in place of ∗ ($a > b$ means "a is greater than b". $a < b$ means "a is less than b").

Q. (i) $(5\times8)+(3\times8) * (13\times2)+(19\times2)$
(ii) $(8\times7)+(8\times5) * (9\times4)+(9\times6)$
(iii) $(3\times9)+(3\times3) * (8\times3)+(8\times2)$
(iv) $(3\times17)+(7\times17) * (10\times8)+(5\times8)$
(v) $(16\times5)+(4\times5) * (3\times10)+(7\times10)$

A. (i) = (ii) > (iii) < (iv) > (v) =.

Developing a method for multiplication

The development of a method for multiplication should arise (as stressed before) from a need to solve a situation.

"How many people can be seated in 8 thirty-five-seater buses?"

The discussion may develop like this:

Suggestions *from class* for solving this situation.

(i) $35+35+35+35+35+35+35+35$

(ii) $8\times(30+5) = (8\times30)+(8\times5) = (8\times3)(10)+(8\times5)$
$(24)(10)+40$
$(24)(10)+(4)(10)$
$(28)(10)\ [24+4 = 28]$

(iii) Placing out materials or perhaps using an abacus, in tens and ones.

$$\begin{array}{rr} 35 = & 30+\ 5 \\ \times 8 & 8 \\ \hline & 240+40 = \underline{280} \end{array}$$

A useful session at this stage can be spent on asking the pupils to see in how many ways they can present examples for illustrating multiplication.

Here are examples:

(i)

 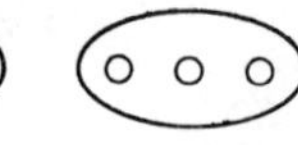 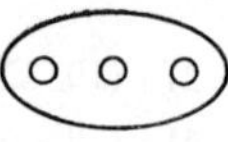

3 sets of 3; 3×3

4 sets of 3; 4×3

(ii) $3+3+3+3$

(iii)

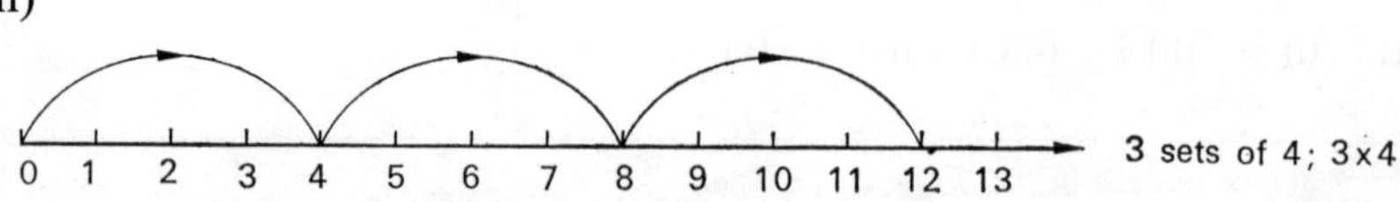

3 sets of 4; 3×4

(iv)

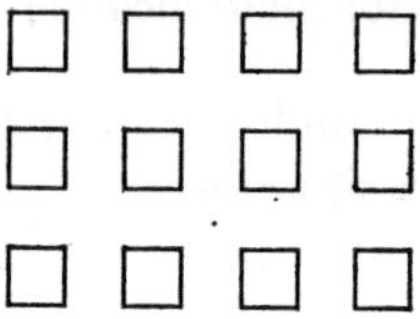

3 sets of 4; 3×4

4 sets of 3; 4×3

(v)

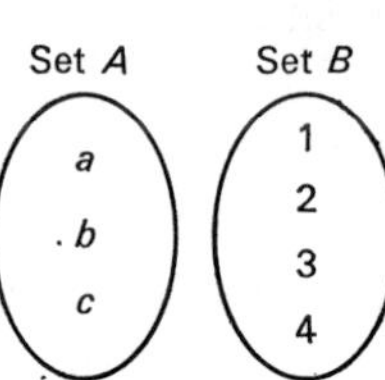

Pairs $(a,1)$, $(a,2)$, $(a,3)$, $(a,4)$

$(b,1)$, $(b,2)$, $(b,3)$, $(b,4)$

$(c,1)$, $(c,2)$, $(c,3)$, $(c,4)$

$n(A) \times n(B) = n(A \times B)$

$3 \times 4 = 12$

Special (vi)

3 sets of 1; $3 \times 1 = 3$

Special (vii)

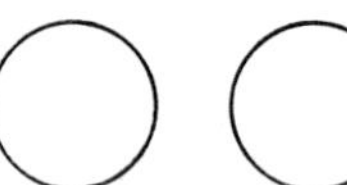 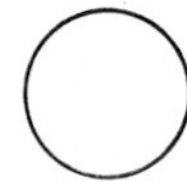

3 sets of 0; $3 \times 0 = 0$

(viii) Find the missing numbers:

(a) 2, 4, 6, □, □, □, 14, □, □, □, □, 24.

(b) 8, 16, □, □, 40, □, □, □, □, 80.

(ix)

1st

2nd

x	0	1	2	3	4	. . .
0					0	
1						
2				6		
3			6			
4						

(The set of whole numbers)

Comment on the entries in order. Complete the table.

(x)

n	$3n$
5	15
8	24

(xi)

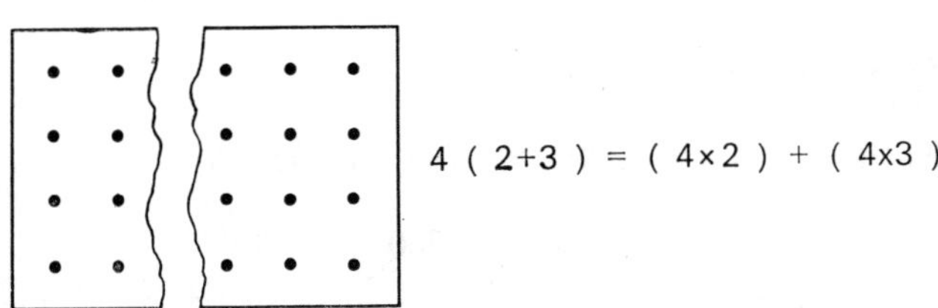

Here are some stages which will be met by children when discussing multiplication and recording. In the early stages these methods will be discovered by children using discs, squares, pebbles, abacus, etc.

(i) $5\times26 = 26\times5$ (*from a situation*)

$$5\times26 \rightarrow 5\times(20+6) \rightarrow (5\times20)+(5\times6)$$

$$\begin{array}{r} 26 \\ \times5 \\ \hline \end{array} \rightarrow \begin{array}{r} 20+\ 6 \\ \times5 \\ \hline 100+30 \end{array} \rightarrow \begin{array}{r} 26 \\ \times5 \\ \hline 30 \\ 100 \\ \hline 130 \end{array} \rightarrow \begin{array}{r} \boxed{1}\,\boxed{3} \\ 26 \\ \times5 \\ \hline 130 \\ \hline \end{array} \rightarrow \begin{array}{r} 26 \\ \times5 \\ \hline 130 \\ \hline \end{array}$$

(a) (b) (c) (d)

(a) Extended form of 26, that is (20+6) is another way of recording 26.

(b) Transferring from (a) to place numerals in *appropriate columns.*

(c) Use of "crutches" when not using 26 in extended form.

(d) "Crutches" entries used mentally.

Warning Again

Care must be taken to ensure pupils do not rely on "crutches". It may be that (c) would not be required if "crutches" were not introduced.

(ii) 365×6 (*from a situation*)

$$(300+60+5)\times6 = (300\times6)+(60\times6)+(5\times6)$$

$$1800 \;+\; 360 \;+\; 30$$

The associative property allows us to record

$$18(100)+3(100)+6(10)+3(10) \quad [360 = 300+60]$$

$$21(100)+9(10)$$

$$\underline{2190}$$

(iii) $86 \times 27 = (7+20) \times (6+80)$ (can be expressed in other ways)

$$7 \times (6+80) + 20 \times (6+80)$$

$$(42+560)+(120+1600)$$

$$602 \quad + \quad 1720$$

$$\underline{2322}$$

$$\begin{array}{r} 86 \\ \times 27 \end{array} \left(\begin{array}{r} 80+\ 6 \\ \times\ 20 \end{array} + \begin{array}{r} 80+\ 6 \\ \times\ 7 \end{array} \right) \rightarrow \begin{array}{r} 86 \\ \times 27 \\ \hline 42 \\ 560 \\ 120 \\ 1600 \\ \hline 2322 \\ \hline \end{array} \rightarrow \begin{array}{r} \boxed{1}\,\boxed{4} \\ 86 \\ \times 27 \\ \hline 602 \\ 1720 \\ \hline 2322 \\ \hline \end{array} \rightarrow \begin{array}{r} 86 \\ \times 27 \\ \hline 602 \\ 1720 \\ \hline 2322 \\ \hline \end{array}$$

$$\underline{1600+120} \quad \underline{560+42}$$

(a) (b) (c) (d)

(See previous example.)

(a) Extending method.
(b) Transferring product of (a).
(c) Using "crutches".
(d) No "crutches"—mental process only.

(iv) $2317 \times 365 = (2000+300+10+7) \times 365$

$$(2000 \times 365)+(300 \times 365)+(10 \times 365)+(7 \times 365)$$

. . . .

Using some of the methods suggested above, calculate

$$\begin{array}{r} 38 \\ \times 5 \\ \hline \end{array} \quad \begin{array}{r} 38 \\ \times 35 \\ \hline \end{array} \quad \begin{array}{r} 385 \\ \times 5 \\ \hline \end{array} \quad \begin{array}{r} 385 \\ \times 15 \\ \hline \end{array} \quad \begin{array}{r} 385 \\ \times 215 \\ \hline \end{array}$$

Try your own examples and use more than one method of recording.

Remember

(80+6) is another way of writing 86.

$5\times(80+6) = (5\times80)+(5\times6)$ illustrates the distributive property of multiplication over addition from the left.

We have been dealing with multiplication using the set of natural numbers. The multiplication of measures examples will involve ideas of division also, and are, therefore, not included here.

Situations which Lead to Discussion of Multiplication

1. Players in a team, number of teams, total number of players?
2. Number of cigarettes in a packet, number of packets, total number of cigarettes?
3. Number of people seated in a row of seats, number of rows, total number of people who can be seated?
4. Trees planted in a row, number of rows, total number of trees planted?
5. Points for a win, number of wins, number of points gained?
6. Copies of the same textbook on a shelf, number of shelves completely full, total number of copies on the shelves?

Discuss carefully every example. (Is it sense or nonsense?)

30 m.p.h. How far in 6 hours? This can be very unreal. (Try it.) Yet an aeroplane *can* fly at a steady 550 m.p.h. for 6 hours.

CHAPTER 9

DIVISION

Defining Division: its Properties

Division can be defined in terms of multiplication.

$$\frac{6}{2} = x \quad \text{can be read as} \quad 2 \times x = 6.$$

"Twice some natural number is another way of writing 6."

$$\frac{18}{6} \rightarrow 6 \times \square = 18. \qquad \frac{49}{7} \rightarrow 7 \times \square = 49.$$

Q. *Write in multiplication form*

$$\frac{56}{7}, \quad \frac{81}{9}, \quad \frac{40}{8}, \quad \frac{54}{9}, \quad \frac{120}{10}, \quad \frac{225}{5}$$

A. $7 \times \square = 56$; $9 \times \square = 81$; $8 \times \square = 40$; $9 \times \square = 54$;
$10 \times \square = 120$; $5 \times \square = 225$.

$\frac{a}{b} = c$ if $b \times c = a$. But b must *not* be zero.

We *cannot* divide by zero.

$\frac{5}{0}$ asks $0 \times \square = 5$. [No number will make this statement true.]

There is nothing unique which can replace $\square$. In fact $\frac{5}{0}$ is meaningless.

$\frac{0}{0}$ asks $0 \times \square = 0$. [Any number will make this statement true.]

Here because any number can replace □, $\frac{0}{0}$ is meaningless.

We can discuss these situations:

We have 16 oranges.
How many sets of 8 can I obtain from the set of 16 oranges?

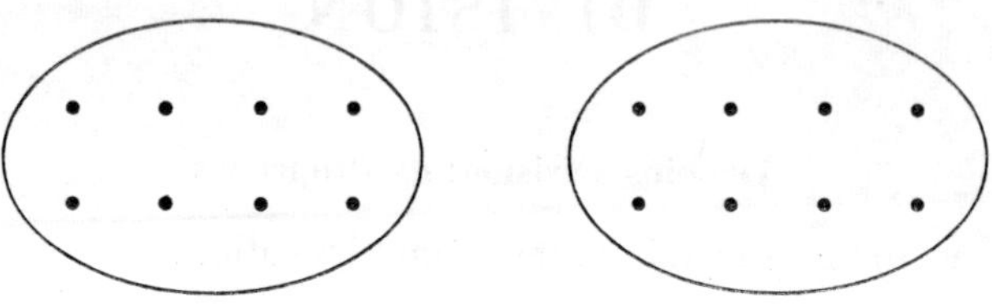

I have partitioned the set of 16 oranges into 2 sets of 8 oranges.

$$\frac{16}{2} = 8 \quad \text{also} \quad 2 \times 8 = 16.$$

Here I know the NUMBER IN EACH SUBSET, (8). I wanted to find the NUMBER OF SUBSETS.

The set of 16 oranges we considered at the beginning is known as the UNIVERSAL set we are considering.

Universal set	24	36	48	60	56	63	72	81	96	120	105	144
Number in a subset	6	12	8	12	7	9	8	9	12	20	5	24
Number of subsets	□	□	□	□	□	□	□	□	□	□	□	□
Solution	4	3	6	5	8	7	9	9	8	10	21	6

We could have looked at these examples another way.

We have 16 oranges. I want 8 subsets. Number of oranges in each subset?

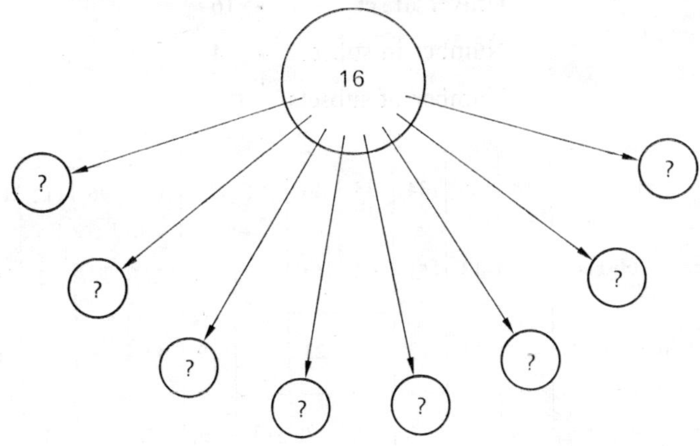

Here I knew the number in the universal set and I want 8 subsets. There will be 2 oranges in each subset.

The situation is:

Number in universal set known. Number of subsets known. Find the number in each subset.

So we have TWO presentations:

(a) Knowing the universal set and the number in a subset find the NUMBER OF SUBSETS.

(b) Knowing the universal set and the number of subsets find the NUMBER IN A SUBSET.

(i) Share 16 oranges equally among 4 children. How many oranges will each child receive?

Universal set	→	16
Subsets	→	4
Number in a subset		□.

(ii) Share 16 oranges among a set of children giving each child 4 oranges. How many children in the set?

Universal set → 16

Number in subset → 4

Number of subsets □.

Universal set	18	26	34	38	46	52	27	69	96	112	120	240
Number of subsets	3	13	□	2	□	4	□	□	12	□	□	□
Number in a subset	□	□	17	□	23	□	9	13	□	14	10	20
Solution	6,	2,	2,	19,	2,	13,	3,	3,	8,	8,	12,	12

STUDY THESE EXAMPLES

4 subsets of 4 from a set of 16

$$\frac{16}{4} = 4$$

$16 = 4 \times 4$

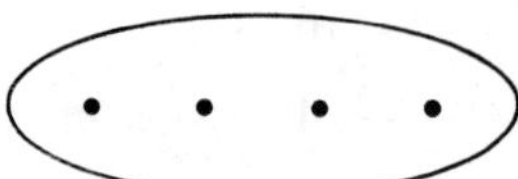

Number of dots to make into an array	20	30	54	84	144	1000	1760
Number in each subset to ring	5	5	9	12	6	200	220
How many subsets formed?	□	□	□	□	□	□	□
Solution	4	6	6	7	24	5	8

Exercises for development purposes.

(i) *Ans.* *Ans.*

How many 8's in 72? (9) $\frac{144}{8} = \square$ (18)

$\frac{72}{9} = \square$ (8) $\frac{96}{12} = \square$ (8)

$\frac{24}{6} = \square$ (4) $\frac{132}{11} = \square$ (12)

$\frac{56}{8} = \square$ (7) $\frac{63}{9} = \square$ (7)

(ii)

Chairs in a hall	800	100	160	120	200	400	600	150	180
Number of rows	20	10	16	□	□	□	□	15	□
Number in each row	□	□	□	12	25	25	30	□	18
Answer	40	10	10	10	8	16	20	10	10

NOTE

(a) Division could be expressed in *terms of subtraction*.
30 chairs altogether, arranged equally with 6 in a row. How many rows?

$$\begin{array}{r} 30 \\ -6 \rightarrow (1) \\ \hline 24 \\ -6 \rightarrow (2) \\ \hline 18 \\ -6 \rightarrow (3) \\ \hline 12 \\ -6 \rightarrow (4) \\ \hline 6 \\ -6 \rightarrow (5) \\ \hline \end{array} \quad 5 \text{ rows}$$

$$\frac{30}{6} = 5 \text{ because } 5 \times 6 = 30.$$

(b) $\frac{36}{7} = \square$. Here the truth set is $\{5\frac{1}{7}\}$.

But $5\frac{1}{7}$ *is not a natural number*. In the set of natural numbers we cannot have $5\frac{1}{7}$, so

$\frac{36}{7}$ is meaningless in the set of natural numbers.

Q. Can I find a non-empty truth set to these open sentences in the set of natural numbers?

$$\frac{16}{4} = \square, \quad \frac{18}{4} = \square, \quad \frac{54}{6} = \square, \quad \frac{64}{6} = \square, \quad \frac{72}{11} = \square, \quad \frac{72}{6} = \square.$$

A. Yes (4). No. Yes (9). No. No. Yes (12).

Summary

We can look at division, to date, as:

(a) *Division and sets*

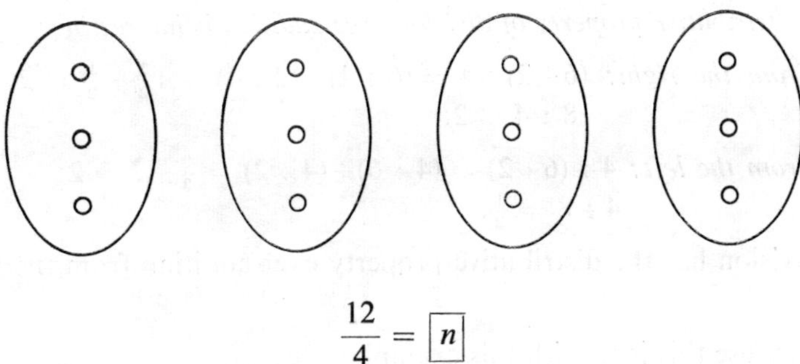

$$\frac{12}{4} = \boxed{n}$$

(b) *Division and multiplication*

$$\frac{12}{4} = \boxed{n} \rightarrow 4 \times \boxed{n} = 12.$$

(c) *Division and subtraction*

$$\frac{12}{4} \rightarrow \begin{array}{r} 12 \\ -4 \\ \hline 8 \\ -4 \\ \hline 4 \\ -4 \end{array} \begin{array}{l} \\ \rightarrow (1) \\ \\ \rightarrow (2) \\ \\ \rightarrow (3) \end{array} \quad \rightarrow 3$$

(d) $\square = \frac{5}{0} \rightarrow 0 \times \square = 5.$ No solution set.

(e) $\square = \frac{0}{0} \rightarrow 0 \times \square = 0.$ Any number will replace. $\frac{0}{0}$ is meaningless.

(f) $\square = \frac{0}{5} \quad 5 \times \square = 0.$ Zero is the solution. Divide zero by any number and the solution set is $\{0\}$.

(g) *Division does not possess the* COMMUTATIVE PROPERTY

$$8 \div 4 \neq 4 \div 8.$$

(h) *Division does not possess the* ASSOCIATIVE PROPERTY

$$12 \div (4 \div 2) \neq (12 \div 4) \div 2.$$

(i) *The distributive property of division over addition is interesting:*

From the right: $(6+2) \div 4 = (6 \div 4)+(2 \div 4) = 1\frac{1}{2}+\frac{1}{2} = 2$
$8 \div 4 = 2.$

From the left: $4 \div (6+2) = (4 \div 6)+(4 \div 2) = \frac{2}{3}+2 = 2\frac{2}{3}$
$4 \div 8 = \frac{1}{2}.$

So division has the distributive property over addition from the *right* only.

We can use this idea with this example:

$$\frac{36}{3} \rightarrow 36 \div 3 \quad (30+6) \div 3 \quad (30 \div 3)+(6 \div 3)$$

$$[(10+2)] \text{ threes}$$
$$\underline{12} \text{ (threes)}$$

OR

Expressing multiplication in terms of subtraction:

$$\begin{array}{rl} 36 & \\ -30 & \rightarrow 10 \text{ threes} \\ \hline 6 & \\ -6 & \rightarrow 2 \text{ threes} \\ \hline & 12 \text{ threes} \end{array}$$

Here are some more examples:

(a) $4\,|\overline{128} \quad 4\,|\,120+8 \quad \frac{30+2}{4\,|\,120+8} = 32$ (fours);

(b) $8\,|\overline{168} \quad 8\,|\,160+8 \quad \frac{20+1}{8\,|\,160+8} = 21$ (eights).

(a) could have been expressed in terms of subtraction:

(i)
```
4 | 128
    -40 → 10 fours
     88
    -40 → 10 fours
     48
    -40 → 10 fours
      8
    - 8 →  2 fours
          32 fours
```

(ii)
```
4 | 128
    -80 → 20 fours
     48
    -40 → 10 fours
      8
    - 8 →  2 fours
          32 fours
```

(iii)
```
       30
4 |   128
     -120 → 30 fours
        8
       -8 →  2 fours
            32 fours
```

Discussion

$$\frac{128}{4} = \square, \quad 4\times\square = 128.$$

$4\,\overline{|128}$ with quotient 32. From this statement, find the solution set to these statements, *without computing on paper*.

$4\times 32 = \square$	(128)	$128 \div 32 = \square$	(4)
$32\times 4 = \square$	(128)	$128 \div 16 = \square$	(8)
		$128 \div 8 = \square$	(16)
		$8 \times 32 = \square$	(256)

Example. Here is an example worked out for you. Make up other examples involving division and multiplication which can be solved *without* *computing on paper.*

```
   56
6|336
 -300 → 50 sixes
   36
  -36 →  6 sixes
        56 sixes
```

Discussing Division in Class

Here are some stages which should be discussed with the class when division is being considered. It is suggested this is the best method to present division after other methods have been discussed.

(i) 3 | 15 — 15 partitioned into 3 subsets.
First we are dealing with *tens*.

3 | 15 — *Will there be any tens in each subset?*
The smallest number of tens in a subset is one ten so $10\times3 = 30$.
But we have only 15 in our universal set, so there are no tens in a subset.
Will there be any ones in a subset?

$1\times3 = 3$
$2\times3 = 6$
$3\times3 = 9$
$4\times3 = 12$
$5\times3 = 15$

```
   5
3|15
  15
```

There are 5 ones in each subset and we have used the 15 in our universal set.

(ii) 5 | 365 — We have 365 in our universal set. We are going to partition the 365 into 5 subsets.

5 | 365 — Our first value is 300. We are concerned with hundreds.

Will there be any hundreds in each subset?

$100\times5 = 500.$

There will be no hundreds in each subset because $500 > 365$.

No hundreds

$5\overline{)365}$

Will there be any tens in each subset?

$10\times5 = 50$
$20\times5 = 100$
$30\times5 = 150$
$40\times5 = 200$
$50\times5 = 250$
$60\times5 = 300$ (getting close)
$70\times5 = 350$ (closer)
$80\times5 = 400$ $(400 > 365)$

$$\begin{array}{r} 70 \\ 5\overline{)365} \\ \underline{350} \\ 15 \end{array}$$

There will be 7 tens in each subset.
We have used 350 of the 365.
Will there be any ones in each subset?

$$\begin{array}{r} \left.\begin{array}{r} 3 \\ 70 \end{array}\right\} 73 \\ 5\overline{)365} \\ \underline{350} \\ 15 \\ \underline{15} \end{array}$$

$1\times5 = 5$
$2\times5 = 10$
$3\times5 = 15$ (Yes)

$\dfrac{365}{5} = 73.$ Also $73\times5 = 365$.

For Special Study

(iii) $88\,|\overline{3520}$

Our universal set is 3520.
We require 88 subsets.
Our first value to consider will be *thousands*.
Will there be any thousands in each subset?

$$1000 \times 88 = 88{,}000$$

No thousands (88,000 > 3520).

$88\,|\overline{3520}$

Will there be any hundreds in each subset?

$$100 \times 88 = 8800.$$

No hundreds 8800 > 3520
Will there be any tens in each subset?

$$\begin{array}{r} 40 \\ 88\,|\overline{3520} \\ \underline{3520} \end{array}$$

$$\begin{aligned} 10 \times 88 &= 880 \\ 20 \times 88 &= 1760 \\ 30 \times 88 &= 2640 \text{ (getting nearer)} \\ 40 \times 88 &= \underline{3520} \text{ (3520 = 3520)} \end{aligned}$$

So $\dfrac{3520}{88} = 40$ (eighty-eights)

$$\begin{aligned} 88 \times 40 &= 3520 \\ 22 \times 160 &= 3520 \\ 3520 \div 176 &= 20 \\ 3520 \div 44 &= 80 \end{aligned}$$

. . . .

. . . .

Make up some examples of your own, and find the solution set using methods suggested.

Note

Although the last three examples appear long-winded, it has been found that pupils will soon omit recording much of the marginal work. They will do these calculations *mentally*.

INDEX